Milwaukee Does Strange Things to People

Susan Firer

New & Selected Poems
1979-2007

D1462254

Also by Susan Firer

My Life With the Tsar and Other Poems, New Rivers Press, 1979
The Underground Communion Rail, West End Press, 1992
The Lives of the Saints and Everything, Cleveland State Poetry Center, 1993
The Laugh We Make When We Fall, The Backwaters Press, 2001

Published by: The Backwaters Press
                     Greg Kosmicki, Editor/Publisher
                     Rich Wyatt, Editor
                     3502 North 52nd Street
                     Omaha, Nebraska 68104-3506

                     thebackwaterspresss@gmail.com
                     www.thebackwaterspress.com

            ISBN: 978-0-9793934-2-6 13 digit
                    0-9793934-2-6 10 digit

Acknowledgements

Some of the poems in this book have appeared in the following magazines.
My thanks to all editors.

The Chicago Review: "Building the House of Crazy," "The Mongolian
   Contortionist with Pigeons," "Phantom Love."
Conduit: "Hello Li Po," "Dear Transport."
Crab Orchard Review: "Pumpkin Seeds."
Cream City Review: "The City of Lake Circles Signs' Small Tornadoes,"
   "For My Sins I Live in Milwaukee," "God Sightings," "The Halo
   Factory," "I, The Excommunicate," "The Lives of the Saints,"
   "Saint Wilgefortis," "Whitman's Voice."
Dreams and Secrets: "My Mother's Garters."
Exquisite Corpse: "Pagan Babies."
Farmer's Market: "Michigan."
Fox Cry Review: "Aoi Matsuri."
Free Verse: "Always," "Life in Waves," "Under the Night Meteor-Shocked
   Sky," "The Undertow," "Wreckage."
The Georgia Review: "Peonies."
Hanging Loose: "Let Us Celebrate," "The Wildlife of Death."
The Heartlands Today: "The Suicide Sister's Dance Hall Heart Visits the
   Romance Factory."
The Iowa Review: 'The Bright Waterfall of Angels," "Lilacs," "A Paper
   Prayer."
Iris: 'The Blue Umbrella Dance."
Jane's Stories II: "Compline."
jubilat: "Hydromancy."
Lungfull!: "Milwaukee," "... , ! . ? #V."
Margie: "The Island of Wingnut Stars," "Last Winter," "The Stars are a
   Lovely Chandelier," "The Star Club Portal."
Milwaukee Magazine: "Milwaukee Does Strange Things to People."
Mothering: "Bay Shore Hosiery."
MS: "My Mothers' Rosaries."
Natural Bridge: "The Butterfly Graveyard."
New American Writing: "... , ! . ? #LV."
North American Review: "Hsuan T'sao."

Many of the poems in this book were performed on "Arts' Place," WMVS-TV (Milwaukee Public Television), "Hotel Milwaukee," WHAD-FM (Wisconsin Public Radio), and "Lake Effect," WUWM (Milwaukee Public Radio). Garrison Keillor read two of these poems on NPR's "Writers' Almanac."

Some of the poems in this book have appeared in the following anthologies. My thanks to all the editors.

The Book of Irish American Poetry: From the Eighteenth Century to the Present, University of Notre Dame Press, 2007.
Fresh Water, Michigan State University Press, 2006.
The Best of the Heartlands: Selections from 15 Years of Midwest Life & Art, The Firelands Writing Center of Bowling Green State University, 2006.
Visiting Frost: Poems Inspired by the Life and Work of Robert Frost, University of Iowa Press, 2005.
Sweeping Beauty: Contemporary Women on Housework, University of Iowa Press, 2005.
In My Neighborhood: Celebrating Wisconsin Cities, Prairie Oak Press, 2000.
To Honor a Teacher, Andrews McMeel Publishing, 1999.
The Talking of Hands: Unpublished Writing by New Rivers Authors, New Rivers Press, 1998.
A Whole Other Ballgame: Women's Literature on Women's Sport, Farrar, Straus and Giroux, 1997.
Diamonds Are a Girl's Best Friend, Faber and Faber, 1994.
The Next Parish Over: A Collection of Irish-American Writing, New Rivers Press, 1993.
The Best American Poetry, Scribner's/Cloth and Macmillan/ Collier Pbk., 1992.
The Boundaries of Twilight: Czecho-Slovak Writing from the New World, New Rivers Press, 1991.
Hummers, Knucklers, and Slow Curves: Contemporary Baseball Poems, University of Illinois Press, 1991.
Mixed Voices: Contemporary Poems About Music, Milkweed Editions, 1991.
This Sporting Life, Milkweed Editions, 1987.

More Golden Apples: A Further Celebration of Women and Sport,
        Papier-Mache Press, 1986.
Gathering Place of the Waters: 30 Milwaukee Poets, 1984.

Special thanks to Janet Lilly, David Lehman, James Lenfestey, Susan Lenfestey, Linda Aschbrenner, Beau Boudreaux, and John Fennell for their friendship, support, and in some cases collaboration. Also thanks to the Wisconsin Arts Board and Art Futures for their support in the writing of this book, and always to Jim Hazard, with whom for 35 years I've shared writing and daily life.

Milwaukee Does Strange Things to People

Milwaukee Does Strange Things to People

(New Poems)

from *My Life with the Tsar and Other Poems* (1979)

from *The Underground Communion Rail* (1992)

from *The Lives of the Saints and Everything* (1993)

from *The Laugh We Make When We Fall* (2002)

For and with thanks to Bill Truesdale, Mary Zane Allen, John Crawford, Leonard Trawick, Greg Kosmicki, and the many other publishers and editors who keep in print books of poetry that make little money yet greatly enrich so many lives.

Hello Li Po

I believe only the dead are experts on mortality,
that a man crossing the 21st Street bridge in fog
will always look lonely,
I believe the French Prose Poet with the video-game name,
I believe Scriabin was a Synesthesiast (sin-es-**thee**-zee-ast)
I believe in the Koan restaurant's doorstep,
that you'll know when to put a door on a house,
a lock on a door,
I believe delphinium is Greek for dolphin,
that true bird's nest soup is make from bird saliva,
that Qianlong (Cheeyen-loong) wrote 44,000 poems,
that Morris Graves tried to paint bird song,
that Ono no Komachi washed a scroll to cleanse
away a rival's text in a poetry contest,
I believe a word is a cupboard,
that she has bungalows in her blood,
that poetry is a large house with many rooms,
that there is nothing better than weather
& that, if we can, we all should avoid a nailgun to the heart.

and to our lips a tiny wave came with a few true words

—Antonio Machado
Translated by Willis Barnstone

Go to the sea, the lake, the tree

—Ted Berrigan, "Sonnet XXXV"

Hydromancy

Life in Waves

Ghoul-hearted, beautiful lawn of water,
the compass of sound brought me.
The orchard sky, the hinge of wave
cocktail-silver-hammered. Waves'
slippage & delicacies & wave wattage
reportage's scrim opacity. Quonset
meretricious waves' winter ice arch,
filled with feathers, bocce balls, & light.
The mammogram lady is sweetened each day
by the many breasts she touches, I
the syntax of water, water's hypnogogic
psalms the rust of memory of breath
scattered. Oh, ideological
informational corrugated…
the compass of sound brought me.

The Butterfly Graveyard

I have grown old in this city, on this lake,
on the banks of words. I've walked
its beautiful cruel chemical lawns
where people bend under invisible knapsacks
of grief, visit their Jeffrey Dahmers & Father Groppis,
with their corner taverns and church bells.
On hot days in Lake Michigan bodies bob & emerge
against horizon-sized ore boat backgrounds.
Ghosty empty plastic bags somersault in lake air,
wind snap catch in trees. The city
is clearer with Calatrava's wings.
Maple seeds make black roofs gold.
The lake is generous with stones
& a horizon of language, tugs & ghostships.
Look! The lake folds over us in our sleep,
drowns us in brave weeping vowels.
Before I was born, I buried people I loved.
In the morning lake a dead father's
yellow, palm-tree-covered bathing trunks,
a dead mother's blue-petalled bathing cap.
In a story from my childhood, one brother
holds an entire sea in his mouth,
while his siblings scavenge the seafloor.
I have always lived on this lake.
It is in my breath.

The City of Lake Circle Signs' Small Tornadoes

Zoloft-Benzedrine skies, blanched skies, smooth flakes of burnt hopes, postdiluvium always evaporable nows, in lilac time, at the rabbit hour great moon operas simmer in rhymed houses, in neon bars, in gold cars and lake altar vestibules. Rust skies: *Goodnightgoodnight.* Alewives' silver sentences prophesize in small wave thuds. On the Rothko horizon rigs & carriers light and disappear, leaving a wake of terror & prayer moving toward shore. The nightlake air is close with flesh, with savageries of alleys, words and churches, with small ceremonies of saffron lights & bullets. Bless night's laundry of dreams that like god, like stars, like ghostships, morning disappear. In marmoreal waveshine, lake keepers nod, know not to interrupt other's breviaries, ashes of night light on their tongues.

The Wave Docent

When lightning had smelled sweet over the zoo of the waves

—Frank O'Hara

"Ash waves; cement waves; waves of waves filled with pears, dust and wind; bully waves; a papal wave, waves of lilacs and folded light; perfumed waves; waves filled with prayers and surfers and chrysanthemums; waves of love and stones; waves of lake trout, perch and pike; umbrella waves; moon-filled waves; summer waves of swallows and herons; mirror waves; graverobber waves; foil waves; nights' plum waves; ancient waves of trilobites' songs; waves of remorse; waves' depository of dreams and bones; holy waves filled with news; nights' crow waves; lace waves; meadow waves; dazzle dump waves; ghost waves; waves of drowning waving right hands; velvet underground rip waves; waves breaking with black pearls, murder, and God; Big Buddha waves; Matroyshka waves; waves' language, anthem; thresholds, society, & ministry; come for the always horizon's standstill inventions (contraptions?) sawtoothed waves."

Interview 21

(ī ĕnz)

All night stars rose from the chimney's fiery rookery:
ions' vocabulary of mindlights' sanctums,
burning gnostic ice, irruptions in snap
shot winds, stars taken from the Infant of Prague's
white-satin cloak and released.
(Facts:) Light does not get old. Nothing
can outrun light. Words in space
travel at 700 MPH. In the lunette of sky
March's magnolia snow doesn't seem to move, all this
dematerializing, shriving & canonizing
in the copyright of waves (waves ©).

(lā i sĭz...)

In the laicization of waves
when they make shore, against
the Chopin-colored sky in lake thud,
the large nest I was watching
started to crawl higher up the tree;
claws appeared from it,
then eyes and scraping sounds.
On the west side of words another

(prōō'dĕ rēēz)

interview with death & all its pruderies.

Audit

November's gold oak-leafed waves slop the pier;
the ancient salmon and trout move towards shore.

Each November it's the same; each November
the healthy fish bring the old and sick in to die.

For two weeks, the long, quick fish swim the length
of the pier, thread the pilings until all the ones

that swim the shore breaking water with tails & fins
have beached & been eaten by gulls, stars, & hawks.

Then the steelhead, coho, brown
trout left return to deep water.

And the trees begin to look like saints in moonlight
and the black walnut fills with cedar waxwings
all balled up against the November winds.

Last Winter

was the winter of snow
and more snow. Already snow
in October, more in November,
the record-breaking 13" day
in December followed by more.
The 13-year-old boy thought
there was solid ice under it.
He fell through into the lake.
The firefighter rescuing him
went under also and had to be
rescued also and also. And also
I thought of the cold past, and
how when I try to go back
and right all the destructions,
I slip under. The boy and his
rescuer went through at the
Whitefish Bay Silver Spring
Lookout. Look out. Hypothermia
slows down every body process;
it's the body trying to hold on.
When my 85-year-old Aunt Virginia
died the first time, she was revived.
When I asked what it was like,
she said, "Strange—it's like
like holding on to nothing."

The Island of Wingnut Stars

The dead visit in old-gray-V-necks,
in bad wigs, & in corners of fuzzy TV lights.
They don't stay long,
as if celestial nightclubs with Y-shaped martini glasses
waited. Like space loss
expands, carrying with it the quantum
energy of nothingness and constellations
of salesgirls with strapped on glitterwings
& pink hats with animal ears.
In the festival of sorrows, I
do the stations of the trees,
read the dictionary of lake blues,
take the communion of stones:
scented stones, name stones,
stones filled with rabbits,
clouds, & Chinese paintings.
The lake breathes stones.
Above young galaxies brighten by gobbling
up stars in their central black holes.
Young boys sleep on cold airing porches.
The dining room table's on fire with geraniums
and lights' runnels of wisdom.
Crows crown trees. Bright
particles of language wire air & breath.

Always

The moon 1 light-second away!
Can the world glimmer
too much? Who made the word
always? Who could believe
in always? Is it only
an accident of chemicals
that keeps us from sliding
off our own dark-energied breath?
Headwinds. I am always saying
my deads' names; now, sometimes
I hear them say mine. The lake
follows me with its crow-click
talk, with its Gertrude Stein waves,
with its Kama Sutra poetries,
and sore wind wilds darting words.
I walk the blue good-bye evening
toward the wonder of movie marquees
and streets like Oakland Ave.,
like Day Street, both of which fall
lightfast into the lake, into
the horizon's microcolors of drowning.

The Stars Are a Lovely Chandelier

The universe it seems will expand forever
and forever faster. I watch it
at the kiwi-colored, wave-writing lake.
Today a continent of goldeneyes
rides the cold January
twilight lipsticked lake.
Your weight contributes approximately
0.000000000000000000000000000000000000003%
(3 octotrigintillionths of one percent)
of the Milky Way's total.
This means stars would revolve slower if you left!
We all walk in the crosshair of light;
the hydrangea, the garden's big-haired girls,
sing back up. Crows too.
Every night I go along the tinworklake line.
In tinsel rain, in timelock nights I drive
past the city's dhow like Calatrava.
The world knows itself in dreams.
Each hour, 3-million miles of new space opens
up between us and the Virgo cluster, 12-million
miles between us and the Pices-Perseus supercluster.
Given that information, what do you make of us all
still crashing into each other, still crashing into ourselves?

Small Altar Moment

, blue yard of water, the plaster sky, ghost sun,
the brain monstrance's burkas of grace,
absence is memory too!
The dead sisters polka in heaven.
(It's hard to keep track of the dead.)
How many skins pain grows. A brain
of hollyhocks (A hollyhock foundry?
A hollyhock foundling!)! My pockets
full of metaphysical money, the always
next bewildering step, & guest breaths,
I work in the rain-battered fields of poetry,
within earshot of the hyperbolic waves,
although soon I'm off to Washington Island
to ride a ferry, to ride Icelandic ponies,
and eat blueberry pancakes before bed,
and sleep beneath glowworm-outlined trees,
letting loose the many knotted breaths.
There I think I will call my heart Norway,
with its long seasons of dark, fjords,
exotic cloudberries, and lack of sputnik
ethics. Yes, call my heart Norway.

Cloud to Cloud Lightning

In light aluminum rains,
an alphabet of herons vowels
a mine of whys,
scarring time's flying words.
Remarkable to claim
the world a word
at a time. (Time changes
time.) A cycloptic
hollyhock periscopes
the distance. Black
walnuts fall, leaving
their hulls' I Ching. A
Chinese whisper of autumn,
starts with rudbeckia. Lake
trees clink light brink twish.
In tympanic pier wave bang
trees ring time. Feral
skyway night water lights
with stars' nickeled plunder
and one owly moon. Silent
boats round bell bouys.
In bagpipe winds, scarab
stones scatter under waves.

Hydromancy

The brink's
of light
(an in fact:
leaking a billion
Blue Chinese gales,
The wear of water's
Ice fields, sheet
What we say
Disappear. It takes
to wash a car
Synaptic rags
sonic logic: art is apart
Polysonic too (birdtalk two:
Wichetywichety
Spring snow
providentially
ice hymns
mattered in fog.

excitatory decimals
in fact
Lake Michigan is
gallons a day!)
fur pirates
icepackslush
ice, cakes. Happy
makes us
two feet of water
away.
lexical bobbins
of a part.
"wichety
chedp dzik.."
museum of wrecks
sad farther
opossum flowers

Expect on Valentine's Day

a bouquet of lake goods
I've been scouring the shore for all year.

Just for you, I collected wave gab, ghostships,
downed pilots' last prayers, December lake surfers,
ice murals, a tree ornamented with Bohemian
waxwings, one paragraph of aspen leaves,
and one-cut-to-fit garment of pewter waves.

I've cushioned each item in
fur that's always on the morning
cliff then folded all in words'
red-Valentine wrappings,

and, like often before, wrote your name and
landlocked state and zip code in lake-blue ink.

Watch for my writing.
Already postal workers are worrying
about my wavy penmanship, water-marked
wrapping, and the sound of scaup, as your
Valentine package works surely towards you.

For My Sins I Live in Milwaukee

For my sins I live in the city of New York.
— Ted Berrigan, "Whitman in Black"

City of empty night buses,
city of wheelchair rapists,
city of drunk postmidnight Catholic rectory parties,
city where more people die of poetry
       than drive-by shootings.
City that dumps billions of gallons of
       sewage into Lake Michigan,
city of swans and swastikas.
City of baronial mansions & inner cities &
       & inner cities' inner cities' cities,
city where a playground covers Jeffrey Dahmer's
       ghosted apartment building,
city of factory ghosts, brewery ghosts,
       socialist party ghosts.
City of blackboard night skies.
City of movie palaces, copper-domed basilica, corner bars,
       ships, foghorns, and church bells.
City where in night lake winds you hear
       old nuns crying for their stolen wimples.

Wave Kabuki

Graphic graphite wind wave smudge
electric lake garden black
lacquer sky mineral air cellar
furnace glow burn grog
cloud vapor bench. Lily lake heart
of downed planes shuffled tin integers.
Ether pond douse
black peak ellipse
theosophical treatises.
Ethereal gravity ruched wave light
horizontal tornadic *gateau-blanc* spray
smoke thump pagoda
outlined absinthe psalm
asphalt laudanum psalm.
Wave rind ice stew
tissue Prokofiev-winded
espalier chainklink sunstrum beveled
aleatoric surface graftings.
Ruthless isomorphism
resplendent displacement
analgesics' headlong brilliant
moveable katabatic pageant's
alluvial gouache bethel!

The Halo Factory

Under the granite clouds, through
the quinine rain and wind
-tree-downed warblers' songs,
a man lopes the chicory
cliff yelling, "Grace,
GRACE." He is running after
Grace. The brain's spunk.
If I were Sunday, I'd ask you
whom you love enough
to elegize: St. Patrick? Tupac?
A country? Your sister?
Hive to sound. Even here
—plashed with waves' poultices,
the cop's words: "I never
saw anyone who wanted to die so badly."
The bulldozed heart writes
its quarries, queries, & quagmires
on the horizon's tarnished waves'
explosive white-dress-flounce blurs
and ships' watermarked steel canvasses.
In the garden, the Immortality
Iris waves, wearing its white-June
-prom-tulle. Small green
maple seeds stencil peace signs
on the wet cement. The silver
maple's gold spinners halo air.

Under the Night Meteor-Shocked Sky

With meteor-glittered skin,
ice-flow zazen lake exhales, &
lightning's deep signature, on
bark spread like carpeting,
I read the shifting
islands of bluebills.
The changing ideograms
of windblown branches,
the asylum of words,
is anything stationary?
A history of memory
floodlights ancient snow,
the vodka sky's blue fog sambas,
and light cached lake stupas.
Above footsteps hemstitched to snow,
sunset's gold nests spill
webs and strings. In the bruised
flyway of words, the clouds' DNA
simmers with stars and gods.
The sky's the color of far.
Each day 50 tons of space
matter falls on earth–
most the size of a particle of sand.

The Undertow

Solar flares & Angelus bells, &
the always bling bling waves–
a word enters the heliosheath
(in 40,000 years it will reach
the next nearest star). What
small world have you thrown
your allegiance to? Tanks
of starboom, Saturn
just south of the gibbous moon,
the trees kneel in moonlight.
Nothing means anything more
than we need it to. Morning
the old man on the cliff does
Tai Chi with swords. Lake
tutored birds fly in the mailslot.
The wearaway of rock writes the world.
The sky muscle drops sandhill cranes
that coming down look like old men
falling from invisible worlds.
Winds polish fears, make them
beautiful. Ice on the tongue of God.
The gab of waves.

Wreckage

The cop stops me: "Did you see
a plane go down?" December
mornings the scaup fly low;
the pier's iced. One Xmas
the lake was already frozen to Michigan.
3 X's since I lived here cars have gunned
it at the cliff's edge. Last summer
the Flight for Life carried the drowned girl
into the Chopin-midnight-blue night sky.
The helicopter blades' *Apocalypse*
Now soundtrack slowly faded.
Taffrail logs, cargo, tonnage,
chime whistles, hog beams,
phantom fleets, brigs, schooners,
bulkers, parents, tugs, freighters,
sisters. Here we build from wreckage.
A smashed pilothouse. A jeweler's sky.

... , ! . ?

#LV
period?
colon?
space?
—Ted Berrigan

In the XXI century we look up a lot more (.) (?) (!)
Every person I spoke to that day used
  prelapsarian in their conversation (!) (?) (.)
The feral word project (.) (?) (!)
How long is a lifetime (!) (?)

How many prisons (!) (?) (...)
Yes, Debussy was a kleptomaniac,
but he stole only green objects (!)
Poetry Hygiene (!) (?)

James Brown's duende ( ) ( ) ( ) ( )
I see through words (.)
Watch your money (.) (???) (!)
A Buddhist Mariachi Band (!) (?) (.)

Which world (?) (??**???)
To achieve the light he needed, Rothko
covered his skylight with a parachute (.)

. . . , ! . ?

#V
period?
colon?
space?
—Ted Berrigan

Are cannibals afraid to live together (?) (!)
cannonballs of petals (?) (!)

what is ours finds us (?) (!)
stand up rectangular (!) (?)

pieces of always
outside night (?) (,) (…)

Brian Wilson & I share that (:) (—)
our childhood homes turned into freeways (!)

Kicked to the curb (?) (!)
What men say (!) (?) (…)

When you choose poverty it is lovelier
than if it chooses you (!)

Poems are ghosts (!) (.)
Janet, do dancers love their bodies (?)

When We Were Through

Our bed filled with lilies
and vowels the color of indigo buntings
and other epiphanic terrors.
We were creating this
plural. We genie polished & stretched
muscles' roses, the origami of
spine and limbs, and rushing breaths.

It seems our job is to disperse
the mind around us–
bolts of sky, cells' silly scribbles,
pergolas of grief. Let bodies
consecrate then disappear, reduce
all to a single vowel
the size of a vole's skull.

Call Me Pier

I have just returned from a visit to my pier
Often I am permitted to return to my pier
For a long time I would go to pier early
So much depends upon a pier
This is an old pier
I celebrate my pier, and what I assume…
I had a pier
There is a certain slant of pier
On woman's first disobedience, and the pier
Christmas won't be Christmas without the pier
I wandered lonely as a pier
Pier was spiteful
–*Hypocrite quai*–
This is just to say I have eaten the pier

Bat Attack

In the whole world only 1 non-vaccinated person is known
to have survived rabies.
Rabies makes you hallucinate.
                   At night   along
the lake shore
bats fly crucifixes above heads.
       Bats fly with their hands.
The girl was bit by a bat while in church!
               In church! St. Patrick's Church in Fond du Lac.
Die Fledermaus is a famous German opera.
The summer I wore a yellow kimono all summer
  (rabies is caused by a bullet-shaped, enveloped RNA virus)
I came back (Scout, Jem, ….
   You understand? He's just
   as dangerous dead as alive!)
   = They need the biting animal's head =
from tennis instruction wearing my yellow kimono
practicing the straight-arm-move
my instructor had just:
"bounce the ball in the center of your racket;
keep your racket parallel (//) to the ground."
                  BATS ARE NOT BLIND
I was bouncing a dead bat in the center of my racket.
  "Seek postexposure prophylaxis (PEP)."
Bats' teeth are small.
"If you wake up and a bat is in your bedroom
               seek PEP."
Silver-haired bats often roost in tree trunks and crevices.
"Bat rabies accounts
for approximately one human death per
              year in the United States."
People cannot CANNOT get rabies from just seeing bats.
  Often bat wings are the color of giraffe tongues.
Often we are lucky & survive some….
  Javan bats have a six-foot wing span!

When my son was young before bed stories, I
imitating Ruth Gordon in *My Bodyguard,*
often batwinged-loud-swooped
into his Little Boy Blue room humming
　　　　Die Fledermaus.
(Who wrote *Die Fledermaus*?
Johann Strauss wrote *Die Fledermaus*!)
BAT ATTACK BAT ATTACK

In the Hour

when moon and sun briefly appear in
the same sky, and the lake
folds in falling lights' radiance,
the sky burial of day's
#214,721st sky blue thought
moves through crow tree
tympanic bone, and lightnings' tattings.
Like sorrow, the pollen
of words covers everything. We
live under the skin of language.
Now, the sisters are delirious words,
ceremonious dust, canonic light.
900 million miles away the Cassini
spacecraft swings into Saturn's orbit
with its many rings and moons.
At least 10,000 ships and 150
Navy planes lie buried under Lake
Michigan. Oh lake feng-shui
of buried planes, prophet waves,
patron stars, sisters' breath,
clamorous winds. Time is
landscape, refluent and ghosted.

Dear Transport

                                         At the end

of the pier,   it is I   waving,   signaling,
my hand an   adjectival   swish   *("a jik 'tI v&l)*
among the pre-   historic   clouds   &
     concrete fish   &   (some of us
  must wave
 at what
 can't be seen)
Strange to be
    to breathe the janglechimeice   murals
  shoes wave full
  frozen dock cleats
      neck's goose periscope

Oh, sail, can you be
     the intelligence of lake
who will tell you: a fortune cookie in the snow: (*Go Ahead With Confidence)*
full level moon
   the borders of   these things
a thread of lightning
     a cork on the pier
     a condom on the pier
snow barratry
when I'm gone

Milwaukee Does Strange Things to People

Where Song Comes From

The Star Acrobats' Cirque du Soleil,
the 23-25 vertebrae in a swan's neck,
dream arsonists, *ardha chandrasana*,
the village west of Warsaw,
Zelazowa wola (ZHEH-lah-ZO-vah VO-la),
where Chopin was born, my sister's
suicide room, the dupioni sky,
silver hair clips, Estabrook pens,
Chinese dragonfruit, Portuguese
blossom sheets, Ricky Ricardo's
ruffled-white-blossom nightclub sleeves,
singing cemeteries, buildings of clouds,
the Italian bicycle team's spinning wheels
circling the Brown Deer concrete velodrome,
the white spellings of seagulls on the noon lake,
the borders of words,
mermen, where light ends,
waves' minarets, dowsing rods,
the body's short joyride,
the 5 feet (5'!) of windpipe tucked
in the keel of the Whooping Crane's breastbone.

Mrs. Post's 6th-Hour English Class

Milwaukee, 1966

Old, white-haired Mrs. Post slippered
her joined and curved 4 fingers into her every
dress' white-laced V-neck. There she

moved her hand metrically up &
down between her freckled breasts
the whole while she read to us.
That day it was Robert Frost.

Reading Frost, by any second
quatrain, Mrs. Post became transported.
Scansion increased her heartbeat.
Spondees visibly shortened her breath.

That hot afternoon we read
"Stopping by Woods on a Snowy
Evening" her recitation
even gave me a slight shiver.

It was summer. Wasps had flown
into our opened classroom windows.
Girls waved hand-folded theme-paper fans;
boys after lunch dozed. The class

had just left the snow-
filled woods on the "darkest evening of the year."
There "the little horse" near the frozen lake
was still shaking his harness bells, &
in the lonely dark the wind was still

blowing. Oh no, now the class was off
to a "yellow wood." Someone was sighing.
It wasn't me. I was lost. I could not keep up,
but I was happily lost in clicking

ice-covered birches, in "magnified apples," in
"domes of heaven." When I finally managed
to catch up, Mrs. Post was in philodendrons.
No, no she wasn't in philodendrons.
She was summing up

"The Road Not Taken": "Phil o soph i cal.
Verrry philosophical." And that was when
she posed the question: "What did Frost mean
'I took the one less traveled by
And that has made all the difference'?"

Now, here, I believe we are close to the moment
where I decide to be a poet. Debbie Siegel,
whose mother–and everyone knows this–
drove the family's mink-colored Impala
into the family's swimming pool
only a week before,

Debbie, who everyone knows never speaks
except in gym class or home economics,
raised her arm and
impatiently waved her hand
as if cleaning a stubborn streak off a window.

Possibly in anticipation of all
post-structural theory, Debbie said,
"It is clear
if the speaker of the poem had traveled
the more traveled road, he would
have ended up at the milkman's. Since
he did not need milk that day,
he took the road less traveled."

What?? Even, even
the most completely uninterested students
perked up then. What was happening?
Mrs. Post's hand flew out of her dress.
Michael Durkin sat up and started sputtering.

Susan O'Toole of the best jumpers and knee socks
was about to try logic. (LOGIC???
What does logic have to do with poetry?)
When the bell prizefight-loud rang,

we all returned to our corners, but, & this
is important: We were not untouched.
Judy Feenburg's black ponytail
whipped her cheeks from her agitated
head swinging as she exited.
And I, I believe, I was changed also.
I left Mrs. Post's room bedraggled
with words and their possibilities
to create hallucinations
        quiet breathing
to create bouquets of confusion
        & feasts of loss

and in Debbie Siegel's case that summer afternoon
to focus attention on syntax and grammar.
Never before in Mrs. Post's class,
or in any other class that I shared with her,
had Debbie ever spoken so well

with such precision, such elaborately
constructed and weirdly considered
comments, and I, for one, have always been
grateful to both Debbie and old, white-haired
Mrs. Post, who had the wisdom,
that afternoon, to allow us to leave her
classroom in such sweet suspension of sense,
which I grew to understand as
only one of the many glittered
costumes of the lively breath-
ful poems I am always
growing to love.

Milwaukee

Robert Burns Square   is a triangle.
Liberace   left.
Lake Michigan   is shrinking.
2 AM dumpsters fill with crutches and snow.
There's a thief stealing all
the St. Francis statues in the city.
Plenty of tubas though, accordions too.
People eat fried cheese, & perch tacos.
Friday nights there's enough tartar
sauce for everyone.

The Crinoline Shrine

Go to the corner of Farwell & Albion
on the lip of downtown Milwaukee.
Go into Closet Classics Resale.
Go through the front patchouli-
incensed, rhinestoned, Guatemalan
decorated front room. Go down the
beaded-sweater, high-heeled, elbowlength
gloved, smoking jacket hung
hall. Enter the last room.
Look up. See the whole ceiling of Easter
colored, stiff-crinoline-layered
petticoats. A whole ceiling!
of grasshopper frappé green,
egg blue, crinoline halfslips.
Do your Easter duty.
Stand under them. Say your prayers.

Summer

A bike on a boat!

The striped bodies of young
  girls who spend summer
  in swimming
  suits.

Pesticides on St. Francis!!??

  "The Frozen Lake
  Polka," again
  only a song.

The night opossum
  knocks down the rainpipe
  with its party
  hat nose.

The aerial artist,
  circus visiting along
  the lake, under the big

top, hanging upside
  down, by her feet, spins
  from a rhinestone barbell.

Small Milwaukee Museums

Anna Freud's desk in Cynthia's upper hall on Newton.
Patrick Kavanagh's burgundy shirt (the one
  he wore to the hospital the last time) in James'
  front room on Park, above the
  tutu store's windows' sunrises of tutus.
A red convertible filled with rain on Prospect.
Mary Nohl's Beach Rd. blue-jewel-eyed
  stone-fish water yard.
Paul Finger's boat house on Cambridge
  (three blocks from where Carl Sandburg lived!).
  (Do get invited to Paul's annual Xmas party.)
Big Bay's early April swan-filled sky.
On Bremen St., Stephen Powers' ziplock bag keeps
  beads ("blue, violet & silver") from Dolly
  Parton's 1984 awards show dress, in
  the very desk he writes Dolly poems on.
In my own Indiana beechwood dresser (middle drawer)
  you'll find Allen Ginsberg's Cornell Sutra T-Shirt.
  (You'd be surprised how small it is!)

The Star Club Portal

Some three-quarters hour after
her last earth breath, long
after she was declared dead,
I changed her clothes. I
enlisted her nurse to help
hold her body in
a sitting position. It was
as if we were playing
together on a summer porch, but
we were together in the hospice's
dim lit room. I took
the string ties of her
washed-thin-flower-sprigged hospital
gown and undid them,
as if they were all that was
between us, and in the candle
of the blue single iris I brought, I
took the gown off the top half of her.
There were the large breasts
I knew so well! Welcome! Welcome!
her mole, the red triangle of skin
where her blouses never
buttoned. I folded
the hospital gown down over
the bottom half of her body
like unhooked overalls. I
worked her arms into the new waiting
cornflower-blue housedress I had
brought her a week before.
"Take it back. I won't live to wear it,"
she had said. I said, "You'll wear it.
You'll see. You'll wear it."
I buttoned the moon-shaped
buttons, that ran from neck to hem,
very slowly over her death.

I patted the empty hip pockets down,
afraid to be done. Then
we were all three on the bed together:
the nurse, my mother's body, and me, like
a slumber party of death. Like the magician
who pull-snaps the tablecloth from underneath
the set table without breaking
a single dish, I pulled her hospital
gown out from under death's
star-scattered housedress.

Recovery

When he could finally come downstairs,
he'd sit in the yard under the silver maple
between the browning lilacs and birdbath.
He sat so still
birds came and bathed,
splashing him with wing spray.

The late afternoon I was cutting peonies
I took arms full of the loose petaled spent
ones, and with the hand and wrist
movement one aspergillum shakes holy
water with, I shook a path of falling
apart peonies to him. Then

I stood above him and shook
loose petals onto him with all
their pink and white tongues of fragrance.
I petaled his white hair and shoulders,
his chest, lap, and thighs, everywhere
I covered him with a shawl of peony petals.

Until dark he sat a magnificent peony sculpture,
a visiting peony god,
a flowering Frankenstein.

Next morning out the kitchen window
in front of the lawn chair where
he had dusk stood to collect himself,
I saw his fallen petal garment's
strange rearranged scatter.

Old Long Since

A neighbor shoots
a huge gold lamé spider firework
up into the sky. Under it,
under his own roof, under
his covers, Steve is
reading Neruda's "Enigmas."
In our own yard, Jim
takes up his moon-lit silver
cornet and plays "Auld Lang Syne."

Our daughters are out in the perfumed
world champagne dancing.
Our son spins in sparklers'
shooting comets' white lightning. Pat is
in Trinidad, dancing the New Year
towards us. Our parents are
all tight tucked into the hard earth,
covered with snow & prayers. Somewhere
the first baby of the year is born.

The years' numbers fall from the night's
black sky. We catch them like party
balloons, wear them like crowns. New numbers
take the place of the old. We
see them through our smoky breath.
The clump birch and dwarf apple are
grounded with bright moonlight
and confetti. The sidewalk
and lawn are a color scatter.

Is it this simple to make magic?
To leave the house in one year
and return minutes later in the next?
Is it this simple to change the world?
To walk like returning

heroes through all the years'
losses, carnage, & gains?

When our hands sting with noise,
& cold, we follow the sparklers' geranium
red smoldering spikes up the hill
to the yellow door of our house.
We leave behind us the horns
& songs, wooden spoons and aluminum
sauce pans & confetti,
which in spring we'll turn into ground
our garden will burst bright from.

Memorial Day

Carefully as place settings,
I arrange bundles of lily-
of-the-valley under each
carved name. I'm
weakened by the flowers'

fragrance filled with saints, dragons,
& crucifixions. My Aunt Virginia,
who is in her 80s, doesn't
care for "the wild plant,
the way it spreads."

The Dutch do. They plant pips of it
in the first garden a
couple owns. Ever after, each
blooming celebrates "the renewal
of love." I place lily-of-the-valley

on my parents' and sisters'
graves. Under each family name
along with the flowers
I arrange small bundles of prayers
and words around loneliness

and loss and breath. I
pull grass grown from them
and tie it with the strong leaves
of the lily-of-the-valley
to take with me.

I am the last of them.
I must straighten and tidy
the small earth of memory
a family tries to keep

with flowers & photos,
carved stones & breath.

Lilac Crime

They are dusting Lake Park's lilacs
for fingerprints. Please
tell no one that you saw me
wearing only dangling
white rhinestone earrings,
Charles Joly lilacs and black
elbow-length evening gloves.

Milwaukee Does Strange Things to People

Look
at the once Mr. Nude America, the now-deceased
Dick Bacon, who sunbathed all 40 below winter
along the lake in a circle of aluminum reflectors.
Listen to Sigmund Snopek's take on Milwaukee:
"Thank God it isn't Cleveland." Maybe
it's the off lake June smell
of alewives, or too many blue-flaming
cocktails & kielbasas, kringles & flowering
onions, church festivals, ethnic festivals,
fireworks, spaetzles & always ships
moving across the horizon. Maybe it's
stone-horse mounted Kosciusko at the ready
for any drive-through fish fry or Saint
Josaphat Basilica's copper dome
marking the horizon. (The Polish Moon
helps everyone locate themselves.)
Maybe it's too many calls to
the city's January pothole hotline
or the way William Ho's gold
foo dogs guard his Chinese New Year
Hong-Kong Dim Sum sign.
Maybe it's the Great Halo above Canfora Bakery
on nights they bake paczkis for Fat Tuesday.
Maybe it's the way Germans
in lederhosen & dirndls gather
in August at Maier Festival Park
to cook 60-foot-long bratwursts.
Maybe it's the way the Coast Guard puts all its surrealsized
bouys tippy on their sides kitty korner
from the Port of Milwaukee. (While at the Port
of Milwaukee, I have to mention how crazy
the whole smelt-fishing crowd has gotten. Completely

Out of Control! Since shore fishing was made illegal
everyone's gone nuts. It used to be so lovely
to walk around the shore fires and watch the fishers
raising and lowering their nets in firelights,
watch them bite the heads off their first live catches.
Now they fish off Jones Island, bring
tents, & TVs, & Smoky Joe grills, loud music–
sometimes do you also question progress?)
In Milwaukee, as many people die of poems
as drive-by shootings. Famous people visit
and remark on the girth of the residents.
The largest girdle ever sold
was sold in Milwaukee. Look,
you don't want me to get all sentimental
and lie to you, do you? I mean
I don't think I'd want to be Mayor
of this place. (You'd always have to eat
too many fried foods at festivals and sing German
& Polish songs. People would expect you
to solve all their problems:
baseball stadiums, graffiti, crime,
which German restaurant
to take visiting dignitaries to.) But I do
want you to know this city
is nicer than you could imagine, even
if *Money* magazine once rated
it 177th in the nation.
Picture this: driving along the lake
cargo ships in the distance, too many
sailboats to count, their sails collecting God
& sun, playing the hometown's own Sammy
Llanas singing Patsy Cline's "Walkin' After Midnight,"
which quite a few Milwaukeeans could tell you
is on the same BoDeans' CD
with other local favorites like "Good
Things," like "Paradise."

Saint Valentine's Day, 1967

My mother said, "What
would make you do it?" when
she heard I spent my freshman
year at college St. Valentine's
evening dancing at Waupun's
prison for the criminally insane.

What made me do it? I do
not know. I saw a signup
sheet on my way to sociology
class, and I signed up.

I didn't know anyone else
on the yellow bus. It was snowing
when we entered the prison gates.
The prison looked like a castle:
turrets, guards, weapons, & walls.

There there were rules first.
Often there are
rules first. We listened. I
listened carefully. In between
dances we were to stand
on opposite sides of the gymnasium.

We were not allowed to dance
twice with the same prisoner. We
were to dance a "decent"
distance from our partner. No one
was to give their last name
or address to anyone else.

This all sounded reasonable.

My epiphany from that night
long ago was: The
criminally insane are not reasonable!!!

The first thing they'd ask: "What's
your last name? Where do you live?"
What would make them do it? I'd think
later, remembering the way they'd pull
my body into theirs, a way no
boy I'd known yet was aware of.

After each dance, most of my partners
would not let go, as if they didn't trust
there'd be another
dance. The guards would reappear:
"Go to your side of the gym." None
of my partners would. It was like musical

chairs: the process of elimination. Each
man they unwrapped from me disappeared.
The ones who stayed whispered awful

things into my ear, which they were
certainly not a "decent" distance from:
"Crowbar…hair…hole…torn…
solitary." Most of them talked sex
slang that I didn't know
had one thing to do with sex

because I was seventeen
& wearing a red-wool, A-line, Saint
Valentine's mini-dress. My dorm
would nominate me for snow carnival
princess the following week, but that night
I was dancing with the criminally insane,

where men smelled like nothing I recognized
and spoke a language I did not know.
The guard, who pried a particularly intense
prisoner from me (think *African Queen:*
Humphrey Bogart pulling leeches
off his body), asked: "How old are you?"

I said, feeling away from home
full grown: "17!" He
looked me over, sucked his lips
and said: "Yeah, well, Miss Seventeen,
you just had yourself a slow dance with Ed Gein."*

* Ed Gein was a notorious Wisconsin murderer and grave robber.

In Morning Sky's White Winds I Walked

I left the house that for days had been full
with winds' strange new songs. On every floor
rattling windows, music coming out of outlets,
out of the places where walls connect. Outside
the world was all movement.
I walked among the wind-flying
papers & plastic bags that wind-full
looked like souls caught in branches.
The wind fat filled my clothes.
It seemed my feet would not hold
to earth. I walked through blowing children,
blue recycle bins, colored gift
wrappings of the just past seasons, &
all the newsprint of the trembling world.
At the lake I stood billowing like any of the earth's
winged things on the border's edge of flight.

Aoi Matsuri

10 large hollyhock blossoms
2 avocados, sliced thin
10 pieces mild cheese, sliced thin
2 cups alfalfa sprouts

I planted the giant flowers
long before I knew they prevented
hurricanes and earthquakes.

I planted them because I saw them
through Margaret Rogers' kitchen window
and thought their flowers were migrating
goldfinches, tanangers, indigo buntings,

and because I remembered Mary Zane Allen
making floating dolls from their
large-as-Ogi-washtub-boat blossoms.

When I planted them I didn't know
Chinese peasants ate their leaves
or that their flowers were a delicacy.

But now, like the Romans, I strew
the *halighoc* leaves & flowers
on my deck floor to repel insect pests,

and share their genus name
Althaea, "that which heals," and
their Anglo-Saxon origin, *halig*
(holy), with anyone who will listen.

Of course honey made from hollyhock
blossoms should be declared a drug
& the plant's mucilaginous juices an opiate.

In Kyoto, every year on May 15,
the ancient *Aoi Matsuri* (hollyhock
festival) takes place. People

in court costumes walk
from the old imperial palace
to two Shinto shrines.

In case, like me, you can't be there,
I've included Denise Diamond's
Hollyhock Sandwich recipe for you.

She suggests laying avocado & cheese
over hollyhock blossoms
& topping with sprouts
& your favorite dressing.

But really, do you think it's possible
to put a hollyhock sandwich together
in an unpleasant way?

Let Us Celebrate

O bed O bed! delicious bed!
—Thomas Hood

where we crawl ex-
        hausted at night to say our donkey prayers
        & refresh our murderous bones,
where we sneak sun-drenched
        naps. (God bless St. Leoba,
        the napping saint, who saw
        naps as helpful to the soul's
        journey.)

Praise beds where we dress in love
        's cassocks and light
        morning candles and drink
        champagne before & after noon.
Praise beds where I first read the Russian authors
        and so many of the poems
        I became
& where at 17 I memorized Poe's "The Raven."

The French word for bed is *lit*
The Spanish word for bed is *cama*
The Latin word for bed is *lectus*
The Irish word for bed is *leaba*
The Pig Latin word for bed is *edbay*

The second day after my 10-year-old son's new bed was delivered he said in
an exhausted voice, "I hope I stop loving it so much soon so I can get out of
it and play." Except for meals and school he could not leave it.

In 1981, in New Orleans, in Hank
and Karen's Pontalba Apartment,
I slept in a just imported from Jakarta
ornately carved poster bed. *It* was to be delivered

to a famous Hollywood movie star the following
week. (I cannot tell
you her name. *You* would
immediately recognize it, & she would probably be
angry I slept in her bed first.)
The bed was a jungle, strange eyes
carved in the posters & headboard stared
all night. Poisoned darts whizzblew through
all those New Orleans dreams.

Bless duvets and sun-
drenched comforters, quilts,
roadbeds, spring beds, bedsprings, water
beds, beds of rice and my much
loved small green-flowered sheets
which my Irish mother packed—and sent me off to college with.

Jean Toomer decided to be a writer
after seeing a picture of Robert Louis Stevenson
writing in bed in a nightshirt & cap.

Bless nightcaps and moonlight & clusters of stars
and lovers, and soft-skinned babies and
old men and women white-haired with grace
and memories all sleeping under the same
nightcaps and moonlight & cluster of stars.

I remember the beds & light & sheets of sand
& sadness & cartoons that each of our
children were conceived on.

I remember my 6-year-old self kneeling
next to my French grandmother's death
bed, next to my sobbing mother, &
30 years later hold my mother's hand
sitting on her death bed while she
took her final breath. And who
will be with me when I the same?

Bless the gourmandise of death,
the gourmandise of dreams,
the gourmandise of beds
and all souls' departing regattas.

Now the last line of defense, the aunties, die
and are taken from their death
beds in pink slips and white, eyelet-trimmed night
gowns and put to flowers.

Bless a day when God on a happy throws sun
all over the bedspread and I think
of St. Aldhelm who it's written
"Hung his hat on a sunbeam."

My slight sister who bunk slept above me
all our childhood years chose to die in her own
house's guest room bed. There
I kissed her for the last time. And
because, except for me, she was the last of that
family and because I knew the brevity of touch
& family, I wanted
to lie next to her
and memorize smell her already disappearing.

Bless brass beds & featherbeds, and autumn's
leaf beds (you think they're leaves
until they fly and sing), and even Anne's
bomb shelter beds.
When Anne gave me a tour of her new
house, I was sad to see the previous
owners, in case of the end of the world,
had thought to install only four

hung with chains from thick concrete blocks
pull down bunks in their basement bomb shelter. Upstairs
they had had artists come & paint yellow and blue songbirds
on the bright walls of their house's many bedrooms.

Shakespeare said, "…How bravely
thou becomest thy bed, fresh lily."
My Aunt Beatrice simply said:
"You made your bed, now sleep in it."

from

My Life With the Tsar and Other Poems

(1979)

Milwaukee Warehouse Fire

the night was red
with the heat of the fire,
the winter river's ice reflected the same.
the men on either side of the river
fought the fire, their faces
black & wet.

& i dreamed our child
left my body
with such heat & push
the sheets started on fire,
orange as autumn flowers
and as sweet smelling.

when the lights are off
& i rub my eyes, it is orange.
i see fields of pumpkins & burning trees.

the fire was long and tall
through the warehouses
& up into the night.

people left their warm houses
to stand on the bridge over the river
& watch
& all their eyes were orange.
children cried to stay up & out,
& men looking from tavern windows
remembered things they'd never known.

we came home to tell our own children
& just then, just like in the movies,
it started to rain–in january
it started to rain.
people who came from everywhere

began to return,
the orange & red colors
running down their cheeks,
their eyes turning back
to their own colors.

him (Picasso)

dressed in a parisian plumber's outfit,
blue overall and pullover,
the year is 1905.
poor,
he lived in a tenement,
shadowy, dirty corridors,
no electricity,
no heat,
one single bed,
2 people to the room.

painting all night, he
slept during the day.
max jacob,
alternate user of the bed,
kept also opposite hours.
when jacob woke in the morning
(to let picasso have a turn at sleep)
his feet tracked across the drawings of night,
leaving footprints,
problems for

art experts years later
spend careful hours
removing those poor footprints
that covered the colors and notions,
the blue and green beggars,
the prostitutes, the sick and
lame, who hungrily held and hold
down the paper, resting
in the blue
period.

one hand on each side of the glass,
it is 1976,

copies of his "cock of liberation"
are hung on the walls of
museums, art centers & homes.
the sunday morning paper
is spread across our living room floor,
opened to an article by his daughter.
"it was 15 years," she says,
"before I realized
he meant no harm
in painting my new shoes."

from

The Underground Communion Rail

(1992)

The Bright Waterfall of Angels

Everywhere that summer there were angels,
hanging over lake piers deflated with prayer,
blowing like soap bubbles past night windows,
flying from the weekend-colored skirts
of young girls. In August, under the full
moon, I walked Oakland Ave., and a night
bus, windows burning yellow with angels, passed.
And still, I could see people praying for more
bird angels, drug angels, kaiser roll angels, money
angels, love angels, health angels, rain angels.
There were angels in movie houses and in sweet corn
stands, and angels who dropped like catalpa
snakes from summer. One angel followed
me into our Chang Cheng Restaurant. Where
were the angels that summer when the neighborhood
women were being hunted and ripped
open like field animals? Or when the man
who walked away from DePaul Rehab gave up
on my garage? When I came home from *The Wizard
of Loneliness* the Flight for Life
helicopter was landing in my front yard.
And a young man was leaning against my garage,
his throat an awful open clown smile.
Rivers and streams of dark blood
ran down the alley. All the children
awakened by the helicopter ran barefoot
and cartoon-pajamed through the actual
blood and night. Mary,
the neighborhood nurse, kept telling
everyone there was a murderer loose.
"No one could do that much damage to themselves.
I'm a nurse, I'm telling you that no one could
do that much damage to themself."
And the police, and firefighters, and pilot,
and attendants, their rubber gloved hands filled

with the moon, and someone held up the knife
the man had used on himself. Off they rolled
him on a cot into the helicopter.
When they took off lighted and loud into the midnight
sky, I saw angels of despair, windfull
and spinning happy on the helicopter blades.
There were angels who wrote their names on leaves,
and show-offs who rode August's tornadoes.
Nights the sky was often a thunder of angels,
a heat lightning sky, where angel wings fit
together in crossword puzzle perfection.
At the State Fair that August, the great
chefs of Wisconsin came to convince the world
of the superior beauty of carved cheese over carved
ice for table centerpieces, and although originally
they had come planning to carve cows and swans,
always the cheddar blocks turned to the gold
cheesy beauty of angels. Angels hid
behind apples, behind goldfinches, hid in foot-high
Mexican stuffed toads who stood forever on
their back legs, their front legs shellacked forever
into playing red-painted concertinas.
And if someone would have come to you as many
years as you are old ago, and told you:
You will be slapped around, a man will cut your
mouth open, only because he says he loves you,
and you will have to give up lovers, before they are,
and children before they are yours;
friends will call you from sexual assault centers
and their stitched-together voices will tell you
things done to them that you will never be able to forget.
Some friends you will bury and children and parents, too.
(Your mother will breathe flowers from her grave;
your father will snore.) Your body's skin and bones
will cartwheel around you, tilt-a-whirl around you
until you are nauseous and dizzy and uncertain.
The money angel will never like you; often
you will sleep with razor blades. Often

you will fall out of the trap door of yourself
and have to climb back up and start over, and
sometimes the angels will help and often they won't,
and you can never count on either. And if someone
had come to you, as many years ago as you are old
right now, and told you all this, and more,
would you sign up for the bright waterfall of angels?
Would you be silent? Would you whisper, or shout:
Bring on the tour, the bright waterfall of angels tour?

Michigan

To live on this lake
is to never go straight
home. My mother taught
me, even if it's only for eggs,
you're out, go, look. I do
for moonrise, transports, mornings'
red lake sun ladders, & white
waves. My parents old
when I was born gave me this lake,
and the lake me. Even
in storms they'd wrap me
in cotton & wool, set me on shore:
the excitement of a hunter's
moon, a beaver moon on
a midnight loud lake. Saint
Cecilia, patron saint of music,
lives in the waves. The magic
of all the lights the lake swallows
and turns back stones and feathers
and bones. When I was seven
an eight-point deer smashed out
of a wave and ran a hand's
distance from all my surprise.
Up the beach, partially covered
in sand, a dead doe. The lake
swallows lights and gives back
deer. Once I found a dead man,
on my lake road. I was driving,
I backed up, looked again, got
out of the car: the startling
stillness of a man's body
lying on a dark road on a 20
below star burst night. Another car
stopped. "Jesus," the driver said,
"go call the police." I drove north.

At the nearest phone, I called. We met
where the body was. It was
gone, the other people too.
My parents are gone, still I go
every day to the lake, send prayers
by crows, and warblers, and lake.
My mother taught me this: Never
go straight home. And already
my daughters know how to overshoot.
From the dark backseat of our midnight
blue car, they yell the names of roads:
Palisades, Bay Ridge, Whitefish Bay,
Fox Point. Each name farther
up the lake, each name farther from home.

My Mother Dried Her Girdle Indoors

My mother's girdle left its imprint:
for hours after it was off her skin, she
was latticed. Like an insane activity
director, her girdle scheduled her days:
"I can't go out now, I don't have my girdle on," or,
"Andy, I've got to get home, this girdle's killing me."
Like crazed rococo interior decorators, the girdles
of my mother's generation rearranged their wearers' insides.

My mother entered hers like a military campaign
in a storm of dusting-powder smoke & jumping jacks.
On hot days, if I knocked on her door, she'd yell,
"Don't come in, I'm putting on my girdle."
I'd peek anyway. What a rhumba! Later, I'd leave
barefoot Arthur Murray cha-cha-cha footprints
in her bedroom's Shalimar-powdered carpeting.

My mother dried her girdle over the shower rod;
it was bigger than the shower curtain.
At home she called it a girdle.
Outside the house, she referred to it as a
foundation.

Leaning across the Marshall Field's counter
after the always gray-haired saleslady asked,
"May I help you?" my mother would always decorously
answer, "Yes, with a foundation."
FOUNDATION,
FOUNDATION.
I thought of religion,
I thought of cement.

1956, the Year My Sister, Using Her Ill Health Once Again, Blackmailed My Parents into an Accordion

My mother even hated
the name of the store where she had to pick it up:
Lo Duca Bros.

She waited until dark
to smuggle it from her Olds Holiday trunk
into our house.

Every time my sister unsnapped
and opened it my mother ducked as if fruit bats
were flying from its pleats.

To my mother the accordion was an immigrant,
one of my father's relatives,
one that didn't speak ENGLISH,
one that was pierogi fat,
that wore a babushka and anklets
to church, one she thought she had
talked him out of writing to.

My sister would go out on my parents' suburban front
lawn between the maple & chinaberry tree
on the even, green, Bay Ridge, well-watered lawn
and practice "Lady of Spain."

My mother imagined the clouds above
her house taking Lawrence Welk cutout shapes
that rained kolackys. Frankie Yankovic
was at her door. THE NEIGHBORS KNEW!
My mother hoped my sister would abandon the accordion
as quickly as she did her charm school, her twirling,
her water ballet and Mamie Eisenhower scrapbook.

My mother dreamt the Six Fat Dutchmen heard
all about her sick daughter and came
and taught her the "Too Fat Polka";
all my father's unrecognized relatives came
from Czechoslovakia to see the Six Fat Dutchmen
and do the Slovenian twirl in twilight
under plastic, electric, Chinese lanterns
strung around my parents'
newly landscaped suburban lot.

My mother bribed my sister away from her accordion
with a trip to New York to visit Uncle Jack, a professor
who taught labor relations at Cornell,
Uncle Jack, my mother's brother. It was what my sister
wanted all along. The accordion was her wardrobe door
to Narnia, New York.

While they were gone the accordion sat alone
as the night convent of Saint Mary of Czestochowa.
The accordion had rows of nubs of wonderful
black buttons. I wasn't big enough to carry it.
It was beauty. I imagined
it vast and pearl as a confessional,
gay as a Polkafest. I sat next to it;
I heard my sister's silent accordion stop playing the past.
It began playing music I didn't know yet. Years later
I'd call it Zydeco and dance to it on sweet, full summer
nights, on side city streets of the future
with holy card beautiful men
who loved nothing more than a woman
with an ear for a good accordion
and all the musics one can make.

A Nightgame in Menominee Park

A night game in Menominee Park
where the ladies hit the large white balls
like stars through the night they roll
like angelfood cake batter folded through devilsfood.
Again, I want to hear the fans' empty beer cans
being crushed–new ones hissing open.
"You're a gun, Anna."
"She can't hit."
"Lay it on."
Oh run swift softball women
under the lights the Kiwanis put in.
Be the wonderful sliding night
animals I remember. Remind me constantly
of human error and redemption.
Hit
ball after ball to the lip of the field
while the lake flies fall like confetti
under the park's night lights.
Sunlight Dairy team, remember me
as you lift your bats,
pump energy into
them bats whirling circular as helicopter
blades above your heads.
Was it the ball Julie on the "Honey B" Tavern team
hit toward my head that made me so soft-
ball crazy that right in the middle of a tune
by Gentleman Jim's Orchestra, here in Bingo/Polka
Heaven at Saint Mary of Czestochowa's annual Kielbasa
Festival, I go homesick for Oshkosh women's softball?
I order another kielbasa and wonder
if Donna will stay on third next game or
again run head-down wild into Menominee homeplate?
Play louder, Gentleman Jim,
Saint Mary of Czestochowa throws a swell festival, but
Oshkosh women's softball–that's the whole other ballgame.

For My Daughters

Erin and Caitlin

I had wanted a kinder world for my daughters;
where their selves didn't have to hide
behind weaknesses, bone
faces stretched tight as drum skins or
painted foolishly as turtles' backs.
Morning walks
in unclaimed moments we learn
to take what the leaves give us
and fight for the rest.

We close down to the spool
of fools that come our way.
Hot summer nights we dress in slips,
bare legs; we are so lovely
together we agree on a ball:
punch–sherbet, ginger ale, orange juice,
delicate powdered sugar cookies,
and chocolates. We all
grab brightly furred animals
and dance to records
under foil-decorated lights.

Let the girls forget the wooden painted
horses allowed in their dreams.
Let them learn to love more complicatedly
colored and breathing real animals of barns & fields.
"Daughters," I whisper,
"be bad women; demand
to be more of yourselves
than anyone will willingly
want you to be."

Estabrook Park, 1986

A ceiling of dragonflies we stood under outlined
by glistening newly hatched mosquitoes.
Estabrook Pond to the left, four deer
in front of us. I was huge: nine
months pregnant covered in white Indian
cotton, holding the small hand of my
flowered eight-year-old daughter.

For twenty minutes, every time I nodded the deer
with the rack would nod and allow me and my
daughter one step closer. It was a long game
of Captain, May I? with deer.
In the humming twilight the dragonflies
dived at the mosquitoes, the mosquitoes
thick in front of us, on and around us
looking like screens on the coming night.

I squeezed my daughter's hand for silence, awe
and control; we were swelling with bites: blood
spots on her cheeks, my ankles, our arms. Still
every time I nodded, the deer nodded and we moved
a step closer. Four feet away from the deer,
and from the road yells, "Jesus, look at that,"
and "Come on." And two boys on silver
bicycles came bumping over the curb, up the grass
and toward us. In seconds, they covered the same
field it had taken us twenty minutes to cross.

Like a blanket folded back, the deer together
turned and disappeared into the thick July green.
Don't ever let anyone tell you
close doesn't count.
We might not always get what we want–
or how we want, but
smelling, hearing the wild breath of it all

holding someone's hand, life knocking within
looking deep at twilight into the wild eyes of it all
and getting permission to approach
should keep us for a long time
out searching and remembering
as much of it as we're able to
like the rustling sound of deer
running away through thick July green.

The Wildlife of Death

—For Andrew Firer

Then the noise in the fireplace.
When you opened the damper the owl,
black from our chimney he'd been nesting in,
flew into the room. You were connected
to the transparent tubes of oxygen
that were your breath that year. You both
looked so strange. Such strange creatures:
the owl so black, frightened and combative
slapping his wings against the celery
colored walls, trying to find a way out.
You, with your long oxygen lines,
trying to get the arched storm
window off so the owl could be chased outside.
Black wing prints smashed all over those walls, that ceiling.
Finally, with a broom you smacked the owl
out the opened window. And you, excited
and exhausted, fell into your blue-green wing
chair. The oxygen lines hissing, pulsing the fight.
Before another winter, you had followed the owl.

Untitled

The handprints on the front sidewalk
were from the previous owners' children.
In winter after shoveling snow
always snow stayed in the depressions
made by the previous owners' children's hands.
It looked like little people had walked
up to their front door on their hands.
Little white hand-shaped impressions
filled with snow.

The bird flew through the open front door;
it had snow on its wings.
It landed in the aqua chair–a big crow,
the size of a chicken. Its covering was the texture
of a black Labrador's coat. A thick
leather collar was around the bird's neck.
A silver chain attached to the collar
led up to the bird's beak. Through the beak was a silver
ring which was the other end of the chain.

The bird sat loud in its strangeness.
We moved from each other toward it;
our hands ready to catch and hold it.
When we were an arm's distance from the bird,
it turned into the loveliest girl child:
thin chestnut wavy hair, a face lit like a night light.
She disappeared before we could touch her.
And that was my dream the winter after the summer
our baby died.

A Paper Prayer

It's a simple world full of crossovers.
—Maxine Kumin

My mother writes from heaven in rain.
She is dropping ivory-painted attic
feather beds and bears' heads,
ice skates and tambourines and monkeys.
Three years ago, my body fat from birth
and confused with my parents' and child's
deaths, a ball of burned-off TV color
lightning came from a soft snow shatter
through my bedroom window and lifted
my new baby boy from my arms. For only
a moment, the lightness and sound of orange
Chinese lantern flowers, then I recognized
my dead mother. Neanderthals buried their
dead in graves lined with flowers. In the Holy
Cross Cemetery the family I was born into
turns into marigolds and lilacs and bones.
This birth week of my dead mother, my son
wakes me in the middle of the night, "Buffalo,
buffalo." His three-year-old voice breaks
into my dream and wakes me smiling.
Like searching through a drawer I riffle
through my fast-disappearing dream and
catch my mother old, white haired, and heavy
carrying the buffalo boy she never met.
His small body hangs halfway down her height;
she is dancing with him, messing his hair. She
still limps. She disappears quickly as a corsage
of dream, an aviary of breath. On the cusp
of dream, on the cusp of moon, I see myself
young and white nightgowned walking deep
at night through the Highland Zoo that surrounded

my French grandmother's house. From the bay
window, my mother calls me back; her voice
is a clarinet. When neon was new,
and every yard was filled with cherry and apple
trees, the plaster saints I lit candles in front of
always had bare feet, and it never rained stones.
Then, my mother on hot nights slept
with her head on a windowsill. Now
a freeway runs through her place
of those dreams. Still within walking
distance, some nights I go and watch
the cars' lights burst shining from black
then disappear into stars,
into peonies, then prayers.

from

The Lives
of the Saints
and
Everything

(1993)

The Lives of the Saints

Wildgoose the boy dies over and over in the autumn
leaves. Each Apache death
louder and more disorganized than the previous.
His sister, my daughter, plays Mozart's
"Divertimento No. 2" in our driveway-parked car.
Behind the windshield she looks like a silent
movie star, her mouth forming silent words:
pizzicato, allegretto, arco. Her violin bent
arm and tilted chin no longer look strange
behind the dashboard where she has insisted
on practicing this summer and fall.
"A room of my own," she calls the front seat.
Autumn's boxelder bug black and orange colors, beets'
reds. (Is there any vegetable that tastes more
like the ground it grows in than beets?)
Every season has its own taste and smell:
autumn is Extreme Unction. The Dairyland Twirlers
practice on the Shorewood high school football
field, their tossed and spinning batons turn to stars,
their tossed and split-legged-costumed bodies
a lovely throw of sequins on twilight. All
early evening under my not yet closed autumn
windows, people hurry walk home through
the confetti, purple-loud leaves. Soon it will be
snow shovel scrape, harps, communion white, and
salters with their orange light topped trucks
spilling blue. But sweet now is this
relic tent of leaves, lighted with all the saints:
Saint Agnes breasts in hand, Saint Antony
ringing bells and riding pigs, my son
and daughter dreaming the wild autumn children
dreams that become their bodies, become the overtures
of their holy, tumultuous, leaf blessed lives.

Bay Shore Hosiery

Clothes have their existence:
they have colors and patterns and forms,
and live deep – far too deep! – in our myths.
—Pablo Neruda

The store was always long and narrow
like a business envelope. No Radio City
Rockette kicking legs on the walls back then.
Quiet colored stockings came in twos,
like husbands and wives. The years
I'm thinking of I was still
below my mother's waist and
would butt her like a white goat
the whole while the saleswoman queried
colors she might want to see: Café
Au Lait? Vanilla Mist?

The boxes on the shelf were thin as
Hershey Bars or secrets. I waited for
the moment when the perfumed saleslady would
stick her fist into the sheer color
stocking and spread her fingers like an open fan,
her always Revlon-red-enameled finger-
nailed hand open and spreading
the stocking to show the color
that would be on my mother's leg.

Always, then, every time, I went sloppy
legged weak, cut from animals,
dusted with promise, blown full
of flowers and dreams. I'd become
a city of lights, every part of me
doing the earth's mathematics.
For a moment, I was a succession
of angels, ball lightning, the earth's
geometry fighting levitation.

Then as quickly as it started, the sales
woman would make another fist
and slide it out of the stocking without
making one snag. My mother would be
taking money out of her fragrant black purse
and swiping my cheek with a crumpled purse Kleenex
and asking me, if, when we got home,
could she peel my sunburned back, please?

My Mother's Garters

were everywhere, rubber
and metal visitations, keyholes,
scatter pins, always
where you least expected them,
like sleep words, crushed
bees, a country fair you
happen on, wild
asparagus, 4
beautiful albino goldfish.

They branded her thighs,
on each side a sore
red question mark, tropical red.
Often, we couldn't leave the house
until someone found one.

Often other women dug in their fragrant
purses and shared one. They were even
on movie house floors, buses, even
in kitchen drawers. They connected

the seen with the unseen.
They were an excursion over white
skin, cherry orchards in blossom,
a gondola ride in summer, peaches,
magnifying glass shaped.

They left a strange stenography;
it said: Look,
these are only women's bodies
splashing geography,

wet as the world. Touch
one, let it run off on you.

My Mothers' Rosaries

Rosaries of night breath,
rosaries of woman smell,
rosaries of dream, spoon
rosaries blue, rosaries of yarn
knots greed rosaries, dandelion
rosaries, dough rosaries,
crystal Slovak rosaries,
baked potato rosaries, cock
hot rosaries, sunflower
yellow rosaries, phone line
rosaries, human hair
rosaries, butterfly blue
rosaries, snow rosaries,
dark cherry red burn rosaries,
say lead rosaries, flour
white first communion rosaries,
lemon rosaries, cold-cock punch
rosaries, confessional dark
water holy rosaries, sweet apple
red rosaries, concertina sweet rosaries,
before bed rosaries, wild
asparagus rosaries, smooth
wood beaded rosaries, see
all the way to heaven rosaries.
Keep me sighted rosaries,
don't let me be pregnant rosaries,
don't let anyone die rosaries,
bring him here rosaries,
keep me sane rosaries,
keep him off me rosaries.
My mothers' rosaries fill
my mouth with dark prayer names:
My name is Susan the Baptist,
daughter of Ruth Lorraine Brophy
whose mother Katherine Boussart

came from Alsace-Lorraine
with an immigrant's trunk
full of women's lost names.

The Acrobats of Death

On the 15th day of my mother's dream morphine,
that said pain was the real dream stuff,
the great trapeze of dead past loves
and family, that she had prayed for earlier,
dropped through the hospital roof.
And my father was the catcher, hanging
from his knees above her fireworks of bedsores
body, dressed in cheap blue trapeze tights and
sequins, swinging his arms above her and
whispering, "Ruth, Ruth." She answered, "Why,
Andrew," and grabbed his swinging, muscled arms,
joined the acrobats of death, joined the God
circus. Her skin-bone body loosened
and fell from her, up she came out
from the old skin into a halo
yellow third world circus satin
bare bottom rope trick leotard.
Her cheeks turned evening red,
her fingernails dusty blue,
her hands wax bean yellow. She was a sunset,
a garden, finally in the God circus. Her
laboring breath turned to John Philip
Sousa music. The tubed scarred body
she played tag with death in
turned to light, turned transparent.
Sea urchin pomanders (straight from the ocean
beds in the English Channel), schaum tortes,
English garden sweet peas, black
shoes with gold buckles, pearl earrings
and necklace, a ukulele, bridge cards,
diamonds, and old photographs
fell from her disappearing.
She was my mother in the time
when mothers were like clothes
lines, and the clothes blowing on them were

filled with children. Then she left
with a fragrance complicated as opium,
complicated as parents and children.

This Big Blue House

When we bought this blue
house, before the mudjacks
laid the sidewalk, I
carefully placed in the ground,
that the cement would cover,
a small berry-red ceramic heart &
a half-dollar size wooden kiss.

It has snowed on them, of course
rained. Rainbows have scumbled
the cement. Children have parachuted
there, and soft animals have rested.
The neighborhood children have traced
& colored their loud silhouettes, and
tongue sized warblers have dropped

songs like wet yellow paint.
When my father was cold
in his casket, hands handcuffed
with rosary beads, I slipped the love
poem we always in life kept from each
other into his gray-death-suit-hip-
pocket. I have also buried my mother,

a child that fell from me, 2 older
sisters, sometimes hope, sometimes joy.
But, then, always,
from the wheelchair of my heart
comes the magic act of the bouquets
we've been, what we'll be, what we've
buried and what we will bury and
walk over and toward. When
you come to my blue house, you walk
over all this, and more.

Phantom Love

Pablo Neruda, what were you doing with
a lap full of orange peels, sitting
in the rust colored stratolounger
that someone, during night, put
into Lake Michigan? You reclining
head back, feet up, catching the white
waves splashing like spaetzels
all around you. I
could hear you reciting "Elephant":
> "Gross innocent
> Saint Elephant
> blessed beast…"

Why a visitation here in the land of Mars
Cheesecastles, knockwurst, headcheese,
sheepshead, Esterhazy Schnitzel,
Great Lakes Dragaway and steak Tartar?
Your eyes smiled daisies when the heavy lady
walking by you looked savagely at her husband
and said, "To hell with deviled eggs."

Pablo, do you, like me, believe
everywhere is beautiful,
and we should try to visit all places
or maybe stay in one place long
enough to know everywhere and one
through it until one is transparent
with butterflies waiting to start
their holy migration to everywhere?

How beneficently you accepted the Moosehead beer
I offered you. I loved our beach volleyball game.
Did you come to me because I used your line on clothes
as an epigraph on the poem I wrote about my mother's
hosiery? Did you come to me to relieve my terrors?

Because we both love Anne Sexton & artichokes?
(Does Anne Sexton read her poems in heaven?)

Did you come to me because we share a belief
in an impure poetry, one soiled and stained
with our "shameful behavior…
vigils and dreams…declarations
of loathing, love…and beasts"?

I took you to the Santa Monica convent to see three
nuns' coats on the convent's clothesline,
each coat blown full and black with God.
On the evening news we
watched together the story of a baby
who that morning had fallen
through a third floor window screen
down three stories to bushes
that caught and held the child unharmed
until her panicked parents reached her.
You told me Lorca's holy dismembered hands
were in the bushes and instantly
I knew it true. Phantom hands.

Under the night's sky cat's cradle of electrical
lines, pink balloon clouds, sprinklers & candles,
we talked of things falling apart
and the beauty as they do,
and after they do,
and before they do.
We decided to go to a concertina bar.
On the way there, I told you about the baseball
pitcher and the pain
he still feels in his amputated arm.
His arm floats in heaven; still it burns
with phantom pain, and I recognize
this phantom pain as the doppelgänger
of the phantom love I carry for all
who are a part of me but gone.

Pablo, Pablo, Pablo,
you left the concertina bar so early,
and I knew not to follow you.
Two peppermint schnapps later, again alone, I left
the bar the single hero of my own
night. I noticed
a spring storm had emptied the trees
of blossoms and littered the patent leather
streets, and ground, and parked cars.
I came to my own blossom covered car,
turned on the car lights, the car wipers:
blossom storm. I drove off in
what looked like some great prehistoric
blossom animal, and I, filled
with concertina music, poems and butterflies,
migrated in the always
flyway of fragrant blossoms and phantom loves.

Pagan Babies

Sister Arleen drew four straight lines |/||,
when she drew a line diagonally through those four
(卌) you got a pagan baby. On the board
pagan babies looked like the turtle totem (🐢)
Chingachgook had tattooed on his chest in *The Last
of the Mohicans*. The nuns
chalked up pagan babies like movie prisoners
counted days on their cells' walls.
Pagan babies cost $5 each. Sister Arleen drew
white chalk pagan baby outlines on the green
blackboard to remind us of our job. OUR JOB,
clearly set forth to us each morning after Mass
while we ate our cold, paper-sack breakfasts,
was to save enough money to buy the most pagan
babies possible (sort of a C.A.R.E. program
for baby souls). I pictured the babies
wearing turbans, jeweled and pierced bodies,
(maybe baby sword swallowers)
colored like sea beans or pumpkins, sleeping
in baby hammocks tied between palm trees
in smoky villages, living under palm fronds.
Buoyed by potential grace, I begged to polish
my mother's silver, wash windows, dust.
In each polished surface I saw another smiling pagan
baby's face. I was Saint Teresa, Saint Agnes,
one of the girls from Fatima, I was Saint Susan,
skipping the Fox Bay Movie Theatre sparkle
sidewalks and aiming for !!PAGAN BABIES!!

And I did it, on my very own, I
earned, and saved, and bought, 10
(卌 卌 卌卌卌 卌卌卌卌 卌卌 卌卌 卌卌)
pagan babies (🐢🐢🐢🐢 🐢🐢 🐢🐢🐢 🐢🐢🐢🐢🐢🐢 🐢🐢). That year
I was 10, I was ironed by Scott Sauer,
who until the very last day of pagan babies

did not have one, not one, line behind his name.
That last morning of pagan babies he breezed
in late (DID NOT make it to Mass), threw $100
($100) on Sister Arleen's always neat desk,
and went back to his own where he folded himself
in for the day. Scott Sauer, the worst boy in the class
(he smoked, snapped older girls' bras, and had already
made out), had bought 20 (twenty) PAGAN BABIES:
(✺✺✺ ✺✺ ✺✺✺✺✺ ✺✺ ✺✺✺ ✺✺ ✺✺✺✺✺ ✺✺)
(Scott's dad owned the local Cadillac dealership;
he always made sure each nun had her own television
during the World Series, which nuns put right up there
with Christmas.) That day still reads
like a math problem to me: at $5 a pagan baby,
Scott, doing nothing on his own, has saved
twenty pagan babies. At the same price, Susan,
working illegally hard for a month, has saved
ten pagan babies–who has more grace? Scott?
or Susan? How much does each one have? Reduce
to a common denominator
and show your process. I couldn't figure it. So,
as I often did in those days, I asked myself, what
would Christopher Columbus do if he were
in my shoes? I knocked back, straightened
my new, white, go-go boots and continued on
the always emigration from self, sailing
star acid lost on DNA & its trailing comet grace.

The Head-Carriers

St. Dionysius was claimed as a cephalophore or headcarrier:
that is, one of the martyrs who was said to have
carried his severed head to his place of burial.

These are the always Halloween: Trick-
or-Treat, these are the beheaded,
who carry their skins like just picked up
dry cleaning, or wine red fall wraps
over their arms, those who ghost
walk towards their lost heads or sex
(or maybe like St. Cadoc, whose main form
of transportation was a cloud, maybe
they cloud ride to find their lost parts),
singing: ALL E ALL E OTTS IN FREE OOO.
I have seen them, these saints with knives
between their legs because of their sex,
with bullets rattling in their pure
skulls because of their skin pigment.
These are the poor who live on the wrong
streets, wear a leather jacket, are
the out of power sex, who are shot
in their dream lovely sleep beds. I
have seen them carrying their blue faces
towards their bodies, like tasteful navy
wrist bags, or like red netted bags of fall
onions. I have seen Saint Agnes carrying
her cut off breasts on a platter,
like black tulip bulbs wanting only dark
and earth and their own buried ribboned
bodies. These are the saints of Burleigh
Street and Center Street, 19th & Walnut
& every other street and sex you'd be
afraid to walk on or in, leaving yellow
outlines of their martyred bodies,
yellow halos, reminding us of the always

sweet luggage of skin and fear, holding us
together, separating us from the always
waiting white flowers, from Saint David's
singing doves, St. Columban's bears,
St. Bernard's beehives & St. Cajetan's
benevolent pawnshops.

Saint Wilgefortis

Like most women saints, she
preferred to be a virgin, "Consecrated
her maidenhood to God," one
big lollipop of love. Her father,
the king of Portugal, had other ideas:
"Darling, you will marry my friend,
the king of Sicily." (What a deal.)
Saint Wilgefortis turned to God.
She prayed white to God, prayed
James Brown loud, Wilson
Pickett sincere until God sent her
a big, black-hairy beard. Beard
happy, she'd run it through the tunnel
of her hand like a magician's silk
scarf trick. She'd shake crumbs
from it after meals. When
the king of Sicily saw her, he
nearly lost his cookies.
Her father had her crucified pronto,
on the spot, one big
bearded X on a cross. She
is the bearded woman on the cross.
(Some people say she looks a lot like
Christ.) In England, she is a.k.a.
Saint Uncumber; English women,
having nowhere else to turn to,
still sneak prayers to her, like 1920's
American women snuck cigarettes, like
contemporary women sneak food. In the loo,
in their gardens, the English women still
knee drop to prayer,
giving Uncumber the whole rotten story
of their troublesome husbands

(who run over them like tar trucks),
and their families, and their
own bearded faces and lives.

Building the House of Crazy

Children's brass knuckles,
the wild God grace of hills,
a stupor of saints,
a cardboard box of snow.
The world often
too hot to touch, shimmering
with cosmic astonishment & palomino
songs. A butterbean bald baby,
the fidgety incense of childhood,
the smell of burning angels.
A woman, me, knocked down in daylight,
for moments a Christmas red punching bag
hung from basement rafters, hit &
slapped by an ugly stink with brown teeth
who smiles and grabs his cock saying,
"How'dja like a mess of this?"
Midnight lake birds fly soap white
in the city's freeway
billboard klieg light showers.
Summer, the season of love & prayer.
Can you float your prayers into the great
nothing, that so often gives us back that:
nothing? Dancing Christmas in saints, I
ask you, did you ever want
to be anything? Knowing
the warped touches of love & God
& the ravines of crazy in our civilizing
cities, I ask you, who will last
touch your certain dead body? Who
will you last touch? Under
summer festival's blue striped tents,
old women Slovene polka together
to the "Blue Skirt Waltz" & I,
on streets with saints' names
(Blvd. St. Michel, St. Paul),

rummage toward their unstrung light,
charting my body's ruptured bilocations.
Backstage of myself, I'm defining beauty,
barefoot in the whisper slipper of saints'
songs. He saw me bruised with hours, a scar,
a whiteout guest of violence,
a certain yellow outline meant for cement.

The Blue Umbrella Dance

I

On this Fat Tuesday, umbrellas
are carrying the people of Milwaukee
like gondolas. I realize I am all
blue today even my brown leather
boots turn blue as Easter
as they dip into puddles. Everyone
looks lovely under an umbrella, no matter
what they are carrying in their pockets.
What makes us want
to put our legs around horses?
Kiss strangers under umbrellas?
Eat mollusks? Care about trilobites?

II

Look, over there, that lady is carrying
a swarm of bees on a crowbar. And next to her
a man yawns under a watermelon frown.
A peacock shivers its eyed tail into an erection
in this garden of bright. In this thick
lake smelt smelling fog let me take you
to the fragrant Douglas fir. We can
make love under its blowing, bowing arms;
it carries the same sweet amnesty
and honesty of umbrellas and birds' nests.
A little boy is carrying his sister's umbrella;
he is breathing under antlers of umbrellas.

III

I think people take on the decorative holiness
of grottoes under umbrellas: stalactites, picnics,
geodes, love-ins, the Holy Family,

Saint Barbara. All over umbrellas
are popping up like kangaroos, coral reefs,
pistols and amusement parks. I smell
popcorn, do you?

IV

From under an amber and blue world
decorated umbrella a startled "ouch."
(Someone's finger has been pinched
in their own umbrella's mechanism.)
And I mumbling about beauty & pain &
love rush over to kiss the slightly
swelling finger. Watch how
in the tunnels of careworn
umbrella softened lights
how easily the fortresses of rain
and love completely collapse.

The Suicide Sister's Dance Hall Heart Visits the Romance Factory

On weekends people dress in snowmobile
suits and ride snowmobiles
to Polynesian restaurants
where miniature paper umbrellas are
the elegance that keeps
them warm on their 40-below-
drunk-wind chill, bar-stopping
snow-mobile rides home.
(Fact: Everyone is overweight.)

The men love each other
more than the women they will spend
their lives with. The men do things
together: kill
deer and drive around
with their bullet-polka-dotted
dead bodies tied to their
car roofs. The deers' tongues
fall from their mouths, slap
against the cars' windows.

Together the guys fish and nail
the fish heads to their garages.
They love cards: poker & sheepshead,
and motors, and guns. At night
they throw bar dice, throw bones. Sometimes,
just for the fun of it, the bartender
has a little, crotchless, black Frederick's
number behind the bar for the winner,
just for the fun of it. The winner will

take it home, wake his sleeping wife
and throw the thing at her. He will be

passed out before she discovers
what it is, that she is too fat
for it, that he is already passed out,
that her crying is louder than his sleep apnea.

Their beautiful translucent children
shave their heads or grow jungle
beautiful wild hair, or shave half
of their heads & grow the rest.
They pierce their noses, pierce their
ears, pierce their tongues, pierce
their nipples, pierce their sexes.
They scald themselves, drink to toxicity,
drive their cars into trees.
They shoot themselves in the divine
search for a tender connection. While
all around us all the world
with its effortless beauty keeps
giving up potatoes & moonlight & birds.

The Mongolian Contortionist with Pigeons

My heart has been broken many times by
people I loved who couldn't find a way.
—Horton Foote

was breath taking, a flesh knot. There were
many fine Czechoslovakian skaters
that Olympic year. Each ended her act,
like a hyphen or parenthesis, lying
on the ice in dramatic, bad American music.
We watched the Olympian skaters Triple Axel
in heaven while L.A. burned a nervous breakdown.
In New Jersey runny eggs were outlawed, but
firearms were allowed. Locally
the smelt fishers didn't register a change:
up & down all night their parachute nets.
Lake Michigan smelled like arithmetic:
fog trees, fog trees, bluets. There were
grocery store epileptics and alphabet
annunciations, and constellations
of life's commonsensical commitments,
the human contracts: godmothers, godlovers
godchildren, godhusbands. And you my
eye-rhyme, twin trick, sister fast
forwarded to death, dropped your skin body
inconsequentially as junk mail into
the planetary mailslot ragbag. You
left a note: The dog needs a walk, & 2
Emily Dickinson poems, peppered with granite
lips. The shepherd, Saint Cuthbert,
from his field, watched angels carry
the bishop, Saint Aidan, in a globe of fire
to heaven. The men who rolled you out of
your house in a Holy Communion white body
bag wore seethrough shower caps & rubber
gloves. The medical examiner was pregnant,

the priest fat. Oh how I head-talk to God
and my love dead. I have never lived 2 days
inside the same body. I have never 2 days
been married to the same man. In my garden,
the red bleeding heart bush made it through
our long winter. The white bleeding heart
didn't. On the blunt end of a heart's foreclosure,
you count flowers; you remember the landscapes
of you.

God Sightings

Will you let me love everything?
What does your trampled body do
under your rough clothes
when violet Morrissey music plays?
Wearing my father's yard gloves,
I dance catalpa drunk in fluted
blossoms and red thrown
from heaven paisley mother kisses,
star eyeglasses, moon crutches, and
botanical playing cards. I'm a
walking genetic junk yard,
a tannery on a hot July
night: light, stink, and noise
from every yellow opened window.
I hate being crushed easily
as a concertina or a star gazing lily.
In this drunk gathering arsonist life,
what do you hide from the flames?
Why the always hurry to dismantle
every fragrant loud miracle?
A rabbit kickboxing a crow, a
tickertape rain clothespin holding
heaven to earth, reminding us of saints
and apples, and the puddle of earth
our jewel bones will rest in.
I have never seen all of God
only the red-glow tip of Her cigarette
on midnight porches and the raspberry
dipped birds, reminders like hula
hoops from Her sweet punctured body to mine

I, the Excommunicate

A trinity, excommunicate, noun,
verb and adjective. I am this
excommunicate doing the God pogo stick
in the blood relics. St. Januarius' glass
phialed blood, housed in the cathedral
at Naples, has liquified and dried
18 times a year for 500 years.
I look like I'm playing God hooky, doing
the God jut, but I'm sitting in the God
furniture, feeling the rope burn of God.
St. Burdoc's mother, Azenor, was thrown
in the sea off Brest in a cask "wherein
she gave birth to Budoc…" (My cousin
Kathy gave birth in a taxi cab.) Five
months later, Azenor & Burdoc "were cast
up, alive and well on the coast of Ireland."
The kicker: the saint makers canonized
Burdoc instead of his mother. I'm playing
the God games. God smells like melting
February, like the flowering miracle,
winter aprons of St. Elizabeth of Hungary,
St. Elizabeth of Portugal, St. Rose
of Viterbo, & St. Germaine of Pibrac.
I am driving the God car. I have put out
my God traps. I am putting out feeder lines
to God: prayer flags, prayers wheels, artichokes,
prayer beads, prayer birds, prayer songs, (do wha
ditty ditty dum ditty yea), prayer words.
Before my Holy Ghost bedtime, I, this completely
perishable excommunicate, am doing the big intimate
grocery shopping with God; look
in our basket: State Fair corn dogs & tater tots.
And after shopping, we're going to do the big
snowy rec room slow dance. St. Joseph
of Copertino, the ecstatic, nicknamed,

"the gaper," frequently levitated.
He was "excluded from much of the daily life
of his order because of the disturbance
caused by his raptures," and I'm shaking
the whole while I'm doing this freefalling
in the irregular wildernesses of God.

from

The Laugh
We Make
When We
Fall

(2002)

Hsuan T'sao

The early July midwest yards
are full of the Dalai Lama-robed flowers;
garages float in their flames.

Before the flowers made their way
along the Oriental Silk Route to here,
pregnant Chinese women wore them
in their gowns "to insure the birth

of sons." I admire
the stems' generosity
of blossoms: always several and

the way the stems reach
past their origin, carrying secrets
up from the dark earth and turning
them to bright-star-filled flowers.

In Spring the Chinese ate daylily buds,
believing them a tonic to lessen grief.
They called the flower *hsuan t'sao*:

"the flower of forgetfulness." They dried
and stored the Viceroy-colored blossoms.
I surround my own summer
table with a slew of the rayed

flowers. In July I serve visitors
exquisite dips in the flowers' edible drug.
Together we eat the delicate rust

blossoms of brevity and forgetfulness.

Pumpkin Seeds

All day they are in the dark of my purse,
shocking against my hip, white
flame-shaped coins,

quiet as nonagenarians,
bright as brainjewels, secret
as a parent's dead body.

After dinner, I go behind the house
to the dark compost pile, where I turn under all
the leftovers: coffee grounds, egg shells, grass
clippings, dead sisters, dandelions.

I turn all into black dirt
and make six twelve-inch mounds of compost.
I cover those with top-soil,

and soak them with collected rainwater.
When the mounds are black wet,
with my index finger, I poke
the small white ghosts

back into the dark wet home-
made dirt. The seeds keep sticking
to my fingers & palms.

At night when I try to fall
asleep, I think the stories of all
I've planted. I think of the small
white ghost seeds sticking to my hands.

The pumpkin seed package says let germinate
for 7-10 days. Then thin to 3 or 4 vines
per mound. The seeds are like magnets;
they pull me to their mounds to watch

for the moment when they'll green push
out of the dark. Not all make it.
After comes the hard as God job of
thinning, deciding which vines live,

which get yanked & shoveled back into
the compost. It took me a long time to be
able to do the necessary thinning out –
removing a few in order to let

the others flourish. Does God tire
of these decisions? Sometimes, like me,
does he make mistakes? Pull a handful
of flowers? The wrong angel-leaved seedling?

Then it's all waiting. I'm Darwinian
about what survives & what doesn't. Pretty
quickly the seedlings lose their angel
leaves & become more complicatedly leaved

& beautifully bright orange flowered.
I love the vines' jubilarian flowers
as much as the pumpkins. I'd plant seeds
for them alone. Whenever

I read a rhapsodic poem, say the dictionary or
Walt Whitman, whenever I see a tended garden,
I can't help it: I always assume the person who
made it has some deep acquaintance with despair.

Lilacs

Before his doctor cut into his
7th cervical disk,
like an old Swede's goat he clumped
climbed the black garage roof next door
thump thump to throw
down on me the lightest, most
fragrant bunches of lilacs. I lusted
for the lilacs, the drunk
lilacs, the purple flabellum,
spodumene, sumptuous benedictional lilacs,
the Nerudian excessive lilacs.
Neruda's desk came to him from a wave
off Isla Negra. "Matilde! Matilde!
My desk! My desk!" he yelled,
spotting the wood in the ocean.
Together Matilde and Neruda
"went down to the beach and sat
on the sand, waiting for a wave
to wash up the wood...."
Neruda placed the wood ocean view
in front of a window and placed
a photo of young Whitman on it &
a photo of old Whitman on it.
How Whitman loved lilacs. You can
smell lilacs when you read Whitman.
Breathing lilacs our house falls dark
around us, drops like night clothing
days' faces. Convalescent-hearted
lilac pilgrims cannot stop breathing
the wet dark lilac nights.
Put a bed of lilacs down
and I will meet you. We will not sleep.
Friends all over are falling.
There are so many ways to fall.
Lilacs offer their transfusions.

In the Houghton Mifflin New
College Edition of the *American Heritage
Dictionary of the English
Language,* on page 757 (like/limb),
they show photos of the perfectly postured
lily & the very well-behaved lily
of the valley. What about lilacs? I write
the editors. What about scratch & sniff lilacs?
All over late May, lilacs like burglars
surround outbuildings,
& houses, & hospitals, & bus stops.
(On your way to your morning
bus, if you stop to pick Gabriel's lilacs
you will miss your bus.)
Lilacs heal lovers'
quarrels, and I swear they floated
the ship from Singapore
anchored outside our Memorial
Day lake breakwater,
making the huge ship look
like a ghost ship,
floating on lilac water. You
already know a lot about a girl
if you see her carrying a sprig of lilacs,
if she tucks a sprig in her hair,
if she bathes in an evening tub
full of lilacs and water.
Night commendatory lilacs brush
the windows with lavender stars
of fragrance. Dirigibles
of lilacs cover us beautifully
as a garden's bell cloche.
I raise my lilac scratched arms
for the mammogram lady.
She arranges my breasts on her
just spray-cleaned plastic plate
like cut flowers. I believe in evening
she might be giving a formal dinner.

So much is conjecture,
subjective, history.
In the Downer Theatre yellow-starred,
emerald-green-tiled ticket booth,
the ticket seller sits like a fortune
teller. She has put a wavy-script sign
in her window. It reads: HOLD ON
TO YOUR MONEY OR IT WILL BLOW AWAY.
It should read: LILACS ARE ALWAYS
LOVELY. They sign pleasure (on our
dark night living
room floor, he surrounds me with lilacs
& whispers, "Now you mustn't move").
Tulips & pumpkins trip me.
I feel misplaced as poodles
in Lake Michigan. Poodles in Lake Michigan!
My mother told me I was mailed to earth
in an envelope of lilacs,
there is not one reason to disbelieve her.
In lilac days, my mouth full
of ripe, yellow starfruit,
I swallow and listen to the already almost
lilium & tomatoes & delphiniums &
the always too brief flowering lilacs.
In the dark I sneak
out on the soft, moon shine yarrow-
yellow-caterpillar-like seed softened
sidewalks. I stand pelted by soft
green maple seed wings that helix fall
wind whip to earth. (In sunlight
the children will split & wear
on their noses the same winged seeds.)
I stand in the ample
lilacs, the only flower with enough
fragrance to convert everyone
in the city to crime.
Dorothy visited the Emerald City. Yearly
I surrender myself to the unrestrained

wash rabble lilacs,
the windy caravan of lilacs,
the narcoleptic steambath
invitation of lilacs.

Driving Home after the Funeral

We stopped outside Lake Geneva.
At a plywood produce stand,
we asked to go out into
the pumpkin field. The 3 of us
stood there in our holy confused lives
in the tripping vines,
among the startling
brilliant shapes and
oranges of pumpkins. Grief
is a toll road, a large field. If you listen
closely, each pumpkin speaks a name.
We stood raw with loss
in the erupting fields of color
under the still warm, late October
sun. (October, the month of rosaries.)
Our feet released the songs of the buried.
We were greedy with loss, grabbing
the pumpkins by their prickly stems,
and loving the pain of it. We stopped
there in the wilderness of loss & pumpkins.
We had just buried your mother.
Our son, & you, & I were the only
people in the weekday pumpkin field.
We were separating
pumpkins from their vines.
We were snapping
the prickly stems
from their tangled vines.
We were taking more than we needed.
We held the pumpkins close to our bodies,
loving their awkward weight & dirt smell.
We held the odd Laurel
& Hardy shaped ones, the movie
starlet perfect ones, the accordion
pleated pumpkins, the green

ones, the candle-flame-colored
ones, the pumpkins that flat leaned
to the dirt they came from, &
the pumpkins that grew lonely
next to the papery cornstalks at the edge
of the field. It was so windy
our hair whipped our faces. It seemed
the wind was blowing the world away. All,
except the pumpkins and us who stood
loss-full, wrapping ourselves around the beautiful
flesh and seeds of autumn
held in the fields of pumpkins.

Eating Pears

Every early fall, when the leaves still hold to the trees,
but when nights start to get cold, & I'm the only one
in the house who still sleeps with full open night
windows, and mornings, sometimes, you can see
your breath leaving your body. Only the stubborn flowers,
mums, asters, foxgloves, and cosmos are still, & the pears,
whose noisy yellow and green growings surround
our summer lives & summer night dreams and spring
love makings, are wrapped in newspaper and
orderly as kindergartners in the cupboard. And
after twilight play, I call in my son
and in the lake falling jump-rope purple,
gold and reds we unwrap two pears with the pleasure
of our favorite holidays (his rightfully his
birthday, mine Fat Tuesday). We wash
the pears as you would a greatly loved child
in a Sunday night bath, when you know soon
the child will tell you he is too old for you to bathe him.
Now we wash and unwrap the pears from all
the inky headlines of the world: ethnic
cleansings and weddings, rapes and princesses,
drug house executions, stock market reports,
rescued children and bombings. We unwrap the pears,
remembering the dreams the spring pear blossoms incensed
through our spring-screened, wide-opened windows.
Once while making love in the afternoon,
the house quiet with schooled children,
and the pear tree at its fragrance peak,
it was difficult to tell the difference
between pear blossom and human
love. We unwrap the pears we will eat,
and I remember the summer when for days
I had to be carried outside and put under
the shade love of trees, and I was fighting
to hold the baby child inside of me,

and the baby was bleeding to be gone,
and he would bring me ice, and water, and lemon,
and one night in screams and tears
he caught from my body the strange small miniature
jelly baby and put her in his hip-jacket pocket
and carried me weak bleeding to the hospital of sorrows
where I dreamt slept for days. Two summers
later just before the pears would be taken
from the tree to our house, we brought
home a new August boy baby, whom I nursed under the song
of pear leaves and the image of too-fat-soon-
to-fall pears, & the birds were all drunk with too much
of the early fallen fermented fruit, and I was drunk
with new child, and full breasts, and Chinese
lanterns that clapped in wind for all such
joys and fullnesses. We unwrap the pears
and the awful summer of confusion
where I sat not knowing myself
whether to follow the what or who,
or stay with whom? I was buried under
deaths: mother's, father's, sisters' deaths wrapped me
like surgical wrap. And who and where would I be
when all their gauzy deaths were removed?
We unwrap the pears like our sweet lives
that grow into beautiful unknown
shapes and colors, and some June fall, wind fall.
Some grow lovely bumped, soft spoiled and awkward.
After the first white slippery bite,
I make you tell me what moment
of the pear's growing you are tasting.
Because you are six, you say, "You
go first." I bite and taste and tell
of eating starlight, and lightning, and the music
of your father's cornet (Hoagy Carmichael's "Stardust")
the late summer night he played outside
the Perseids star showers and him 11 P.M.
playing outside because the summer house was
too hot to enter & there was no lake breeze,

& we sat sweaty wet in our bathing suits & the lights
of the many candles we surround ourselves in.
And now I'm telling you that I'm eating all
the lights: the alley lit by streetlight light,
music & starlight, & lightning & candle
of that night. We bite again.
You tell me that you taste raccoon dreams
from the night the raccoons climbed up the tree
and hung their tails Davy Crockett hat-like down
through the lush leaves and starting pears.
Your memory makes me taste the song of the migrating
flock of yellow warblers that June rested in the tree.
Because you are 6, I do not tell you
but I even taste the February
pear tree of the ice frozen world, night
of my 45-year-old sister's death,
when there was not one leaf, not one pear.
All the world was frozen and covered empty,
like the pear tree that screamed the empty
inside of a mouth in an Edvard Munch painting terror.
Bix, together we are eating the hysterically clean hearts
of pears, which get sweeter & sweeter as they age.
I am 44. Soon I will be 45. The cupboard is filled
with carefully wrapped pears. We are sharing
the slippery hard first bites. We are eating pears
& our lives. We are memorizing the lives of pears
together at the now night table we eat from.
You are 6. You are good at this. You tell me:
"A pear tastes nothing like it looks."
And together we blind bite, we eat our way
into the many stories of pears.

Compline

In snow we are larger than our bodies.
        On our backs,
doing horizontal jumping
        jacks, we imprint our origin.
Looking up we don't want
        to leave the satin-
creased skirts of snow.
        My son still thinks
it's only play this waiting until dark to go out
        & press our original body
outlines in streetlight-lit pastures of snow.

He jokes: "Here is an abstract art angel."
        Then he falls
on his side, roots with his red-&-black checkered
        earflapped hat,
and moves his legs in scissors
runs, like a dreaming dog's sleep dream chase.
        I think we're all born
with this body memory. Even if no one ever taught us,
        we'd find ourselves,
as if in praise, allowing ourselves to fall
        backwards and
let our bodies' pregenetic body memory direct us.

We love snow because it is generous,
        decorative, excessive,
and motherly when we fall,
        & we do
trustingly fall back into it,
        through history,
which is time and human, through
        our mother's and father's
        bodies & the bodies
of the mother & father before them.

Sometimes my son & I hold hands & fall back
          together, like skyjumpers.
Other times we watch the critical
          beauty of each other's
effort set again toward only beauty
          toward looking up & accepting
          the lake winds & pelting
snow. We leave our bodies'
          gratitude in snow.

Candlemas

Out in the winter garden
there's only this survivor of blizzards:
the snowdrop, *galanthus nivalis,*
ancient altar scatter, milkflower,

the lonely-as-Jesus flower
with all its survivor ecstasies.

The French called the flower *perce-neige,*
        piercing the snow.
The ancients made amulets
        of its white-belled tepals.

Who wouldn't?
A flower that survives repeated late-heavy snows
then takes on and makes lovely
the color of what it survives.

Whitman's Voice

He does not sing the poem like Yeats
reciting "The Lake Isle of Innisfree"; he
simply continent speaks each word, & in between
each bump on the wax cylinder recording
Thomas Edison made of Whitman in 1890,
you hear another Whitman.

You hear Whitman
        interviewing P.T. Barnum,
        with Tom Thumb & the orangutan,
        Mlle. Jane, in the background.
You hear all the gaslight
        drenched operas he attended
        & even smell the peculiar
        19th century perfumes.
You hear Whitman's
        body kicks & swim splash & cold water scrubs
        at Gray's Swimming Bath at the bottom
        of Fulton Street, and
You hear him
        at the corner of Fulton & Cranberry Streets
        in the Rome brothers' print shop
        setting the type for the first
        Leaves of Grass.
You hear all
        the Nor'easters he sat outside through
        under his tree in the healing country
        under his gray wool blanket
        recovering from a stroke, and
You can even hear the Civil War
        hospital kisses he soft lip-pressed on the often
        never-shaved cheeks of the dying
        soldiers he nursed.
You hear him ask them: "Stamps?

Licorice?
Can I write a letter home for you?"

And in his American-formed voice inflected with canaries,
          locomotives, and turkeys,
          you hear electricity & his wild throat
          muscles. Each syllable is a tableau:
Six-year-old Walter in the arms of Lafayette,
young teacher Walter playing baseball with his students,
Whitman at Poe's reburial in Baltimore
          (the only literary figure to attend),
          Walter in Brooklyn purchasing his first
          silver watch, gold pencil, frock coat,
          & loud singing on top an omnibus
          in New York.
You see Whitman in the Astor Library
          blowy from the ferry, a copy of *Consuelo*
          in his hands, a bit of George Sand's
          cigar smoke about his ears & beard.
          You see coffee & beefsteak eating Walt &
          1857 hard pressed for money Walt
          watching his Talbot painting and his
          few other belongings taken by lawyers
          & carried out & through the streets–
          all for a $200 debt.
You see Walt visiting
          with brown velvet-suited Oscar
          Wilde, with Longfellow, with Thoreau,
          &, of course, with Emerson.
There's Walt swimming & loping at Coney Island
          & writing: "The polka increases in popularity,"
          & even (I am *not* making this up) walking
          & loving walking the streets of Milwaukee!
You see nude sun-bathed, mud-bathed lame Walt
          at Timber Creek wrestling with saplings
          trying to strengthen his stroke-weakened
          arms & legs.
You even see old white-bearded Whitman

napping in his wheelchair
in front of his Mickle Street Camden window,
like a "great old Angora Tom,"
like a snowy owl.

And in each syllable, you hear transformation.
You hear his dream
breath, his sighs
as he studies the night
sky patterns, hieroglyphics,
phrenology, & lexicology.
You hear him call through the centuries
to all his young apprentices: "Hen,
oh, why, Hen."
And if you are very still when listening,
you can hear him rubbing lilacs
in his beautiful, white beard, & I swear,
you can hear him swallow a strawberry.

Here, on my CD made from Edison's wax cylinders
is sapling planting Walt,
America's great slang coloratura
word hero, plainly speaking; venerable Walt
saying his hymn of vowels & consonants.
And really his voice is much like the Long Island
pond and spring water he wrote about:
"The water itself has a character of its own,"
said Whitman, "It is deliciously sweet
–it almost has a flavor."

Bathing with Birds

After dinner all the open Chang-Cheng,
white carry-out container tops
looked like origami cranes.
In the garden the toads
pulled their finished skins off
delicately as evening gloves.
The lake wrote
contracts of chrome spume glint.
While I soaked,
birds sharpened their beaks
on the windowsill like you would knives
on the evening of a holiday.
The night sky filled with Chagall
topsy-turvy floating men & women.
I had never bathed with birds before.
I couldn't take my eyes off the emperorish
cardinal, the way he spread his tomato-colored
tail feathers in fortunes. The starling's
lovely wing spray felt like small February hailstones,
the gravel of ground gemstones.
I thought of St. Michael's armor
turning to feathers. St. Francis and St. Clare
finally delivering their bodies to one another.
The tantric wing-spread movement,
the song moans,
beaks decorated and softened
with petals of daffodils,
the cello-music of their throats,
the blue slapping of coverts and primaries—
feathers floating in bathwater,
on the bed, in air.
I opened the bathing room's window—
below a black-mini-skirted,
red-high-heeled man ran
under the powerlines, through

the lilac-wallpapered alley,
wearing a red hat which greatly
resembled the Buddha's
cranial bump flame of wisdom.

Peonies

The young girls walk by looking like wedding
cakes, art nouveau vases. They are
wearing only peonies. Exhausted
from wearing beauty, they night hurry
home to pull the flowers over their heads.
They learn that once you wear
a dress of peonies, your skin is forever
fragranced with the flowers' operatic sweet sadness. All
over the early June city, collapsed dresses of peonies
still as rugs incense bedrooms. Wild
canaries fly from the dresses' peony-scented puddles
and sing about the sleeping girls.

Have you heard the peonies' glossolalia?
Have you ever watched a black swallowtail's
gold and sky-blue pierced wings rearranged
by 44 mph winds, while it holds
to a Festiva Maxima Blush peony,
all the while maintaining all
its delicate migrating strength?
Have you seen your neighbor,
white-nightgowned, stop
the morning of her death
to bring greedily to her
face one last time the fragrance
of her greatly loved white Le Jours?

Looking at the sleeping newborn
in its white bassinet, one
would never believe, even if told in great detail,
what will happen to that infant during its life.
Or, if one did believe, one might go mad
with fast forwarded beauty, boredom, and terror.
Looking at the tight small gumball bud, it is
difficult to imagine the coming unfurling,

the coming foliage, the slow-opening beauty,
the insane fragrance. I watch
the drunk crazy ants come like explorers
to travel the tight white and green globes,
the holy-trinity-leaved peony buds.

All over the city, around paint-chipped garages,
around perfectly painted garages,
separating lot lines,
tied to dooryard black-iron railings,
on pillowcases and beds,
holding up houses,
in vases surrounding baths,
in the convent's oddly upright manacled bunches,
in under birdbath heavy collapsed bunches,
in vacant lots, and
reflected in witching balls,
peonies bow with fragrance
and all such burdens of beauty.

It is not hard to understand why my
immigrant grandmothers, both
the tall elegant French one and
the sweet doughy Czechoslovakian one,
prized their Limoges and cutglass
dishes and peonies equally,
why they carried to their American homes
the promise-heavy flowers,
why they opened the soil around their new
homes and planted all the sweet
possible peonies they could find sun for,
nor why when

my mother married and moved to the new
wilderness of the suburbs she
carried the newspaper-wrapped dream
peonies with her. And I,
second generation on each family side,

have planted double-flowered Longfellow peonies
and Mrs. Franklin D. Roosevelt peonies and
Avalanche peonies all along my front steps
just so that you June visiting
might breathe in all the flowers' information,
longevity, and mad medicinal genius.

My neighbor planted her entire front yard in peonies.
In June, I am disabled with the wild sweet smell.
I cannot sleep. Breathing in the peonies' fragrance
it is easy to understand why people wallpaper
their bedrooms with peonies, perfectly preserve
them under glass bells, try to replicate
their smell in perfumes & in house sprays,
and sleep under peony-decorated comforters.
No dreams are as wonderful as dreams
had after breathing in Queen of Hamburg peonies.
After I've breathed in nights of the truth-drug flowers,
ask me and I will tell you
about women's body memories, about
the slow, moist-opening
of peonies, the ruffled silk slippery dark
-red petals, the ant licked
open peonies, the wealthy smell of nights
of peonies that dream and swell, grow
from tightness to wild reckless
loud unfurled dropping petals.

Have you ever rubbed a peony petal
between your thumb and index finger?
It is smoother than magnolia
tongues, sweeter than yellow cake,
better than any Chinese potion.
Put a peony in your hair–
you will not be disappointed
with the suggestions whispered in your ear.

Tong Yen Gai

San Francisco

The funeral procession moved past the Dragon Seed,
past the Ching Chong Dong Building, past the Buddha
Bar. The Mortuary Band march-played over
the Sunday voices of commerce and pleasure.
At all places that had been important to the dead man
the chief mourners climbed out of their limousines
"to bow three times before the open hearse
as the funeral director clapped three times
to alert the drowsy spirit" to look around
one last time. The photo on top of the hearse
was of a smiling young man.
Behind the mourners a merchant's hand
stirred a large box of live frogs.
The air was full with the fresh fish, crab,
duck, and hosed down sidewalk smells.
I had been looking at bonsai trees and lucky,
ribbon-wrapped bamboo sticks, the spiky
awkward durian, & porcelain erotic statues
(late Qing period), chrysanthemum teas,
brocade wrapped chopblocks and blue watercovered
moon stones. Off in the distance
the philanthropic smell of the Pacific Ocean. A small
boy ran by in a bright blue wisdom hat.
The store windows were full of medicinal
roots and herbs. At a traditional
Chinese funeral one should "bow 3 times
before the coffin, light a stick of incense,
and suck a piece of candy provided
to wash away the bitterness." I rested
in front of Quang Xoung Foods.
Someone in the funeral procession released
hands full of white prayer papers.
The wind covered me with them.
They were the size of opera tickets.

Before dark I still wanted to see
Beniamino Bufano's statue of Sun Yat-Sen,
I wanted to get to the Sue Hing Benevolent Association.
I wanted to climb to the top floor Tien Hau Temple
of the Goddess of Heaven, protectoress of all sojourners.

The Beautiful Pain of Too Much

In the scruffle tremble
world my heart is
cake batter. The world rattles
like a piggy bank.
Have you remembered
why you're here?
In birdheaven humans wake
in their dark houses
& lean out opened windows
to choir sing mornings to nested birds.
I am trying to tell you something
about night games,
about the soul's regattas,
and the weight of skin.
Have you ever done anything beautiful?
Beautiful as a man carrying
a French horn? My heart
closes like an automatic garage door,
opens like a drawbridge.
We are so perfect,
so many want pretty.
We are jewel eaters,
children in bright swimming
suits crucifix falling
into Windex blue days.
Priestesses of Incan temples
wore gold sunflower medallions.
We eat sunflowers,
sit on chairs upholstered
with stars. Can you only balance
alone? In the depathologizing quiet,
in the pharmacology of lake,
disks of us fall, human foliose,
into the earth's green pleats.
Our spines light with fireflies.

Our hands memorize.
The body memorizes
the places of rapture,
the assemblies of devotions:
the music of cold
trees, a lisp of ice,
the butterfly forest
(Have you ever put a butterfly
in your mouth?), the aspirin sun,
our time-lapse bodies,
snow fences blown wild
with the foreign language of leaves.
The memorizing foot repeatedly
puts its steps of divination
to the fragrant dreaming earth.

About the Poet

Susan Firer grew up along the western shore of Lake Michigan, where she now lives, writes, and works. She is the author of four previous books of poetry. Her third book, *The Lives of the Saints and Everything,* won the Cleveland State Poetry Prize and the Posner Award. Her fourth book, *The Laugh We Make When We Fall,* won the Backwaters Prize. Her work has appeared in numerous magazine and anthologies, including *The Best American Poetry, The Georgia Review, New American Writing, Prairie Schooner, Chicago Review, the Iowa Review, Lungfull!, jubilat, Court Green,* and others. For many years she worked with the Great Lakes Poem Band, a collaborative effort joining poems and music. Recently, two of her poems were used as texts for pieces choreographed by Janet Lilly and performed at St. Mark's in the Bowery.